THE EXECUTION EDGE

How CEOs can harness trust for unstoppable Strategy Execution

SHWETA KUMAR

This book is dedicated with deepest love and affection

*To the three who make up my deepest trust
circle - Ravi, Siddharth and Aditi, thank you for holding
the fort while I found the words.*

To my parents - who taught me to fly.

*To my clients - this book carries your questions,
your courage, your quiet wars, and your fiercest hopes.*

*And to trust itself - for being the bridge
between intention and impact.*

Contents

Foreword

Great leaders do more than drive results—they create the conditions for their teams to thrive. In my years of coaching top executives, I have seen that the highest-performing leaders are not just intelligent strategists but masters of trust-building. Without trust, execution suffers, culture weakens, and organizations struggle to sustain momentum.

Shweta has written a powerful book that brings these truths to life. With a compelling blend of research, executive insights, and practical frameworks, this book offers a roadmap for CEOs to cultivate trust as the foundation of execution success. It is a must-read for leaders committed to not only delivering results but doing so in a way that strengthens their teams and organizations for the long haul. I highly recommend it.

John Mattone

Introduction

The Hidden Multiplier of Strategy Execution: Why Brilliant CEOs Still Fail at Strategy Execution

"70% of strategies fail—not due to poor planning, but poor execution."

CEOs don't fail due to a lack of intelligence, resources, or ambition; they fail because execution isn't just about getting things done—it's about getting them done through people.

And people don't execute in a vacuum. They execute within systems of trust—or the lack thereof.

The brutal truth? Many leaders unknowingly manage their organizations into failure by focusing too much on accountability while neglecting cohesion—or by building an organization that "feels good" but lacks the rigor to deliver.

The best CEOs understand this: Strategy without trust is just theory. Execution without trust is chaos.

This book reveals System Trust—the hidden multiplier that determines whether your leadership translates into results. And at the core of System Trust are trust amplifiers—forces that, when leveraged correctly, drive strategy from intention to impact.

From High-Performance Illusions to Sustainable Execution

In 1999, I walked into Arthur Andersen's Mumbai office—a temple to meritocracy. We were the chosen ones, handpicked for our brilliance. Strategy consultants redesigned entire industries between sips of coffee. Financial wizards conjured billion-dollar models with the confidence of oracles.

On the surface, we had it all. The best minds. The best data. The best frameworks.

Yet, beneath the polished floors lay fault lines—subtle but widening.

Meetings were intellectual fireworks, but decisions lacked follow-through. Everyone optimized their own brilliance, but collective execution faltered. We weren't a high-performance team; we were parallel players in a disjointed orchestra.

Then Enron collapsed. And with it, Arthur Andersen.

What should have been a warning shot for businesses became an autopsy of leadership failure. Enron wasn't just a case of financial fraud; it was a case study of how trust—when systemically ignored—can rot even the most brilliant organizations from within.

I saw firsthand that the companies that survived weren't necessarily the smartest. They were the ones where trust was designed into the system, where leaders balanced cohesion with accountability, and where people could call out risks before they became disasters.

That's when it hit me: System Trust isn't a soft skill—it's the foundation of execution.

The CEO's Execution Toolkit – Asking the right questions

Through my research, I found that System Trust isn't built on gut feel or charisma—it's engineered. Companies that execute consistently well ask themselves the right questions to create an environment where strategy turns into results.

1. Clarity Before Certainty

   Execution stalls when teams second-guess decisions. The best leaders provide just enough clarity to move forward—even in uncertainty.

   - *Question for CEOs: Are my leaders hesitating because they lack clarity or because they fear making the wrong move?*

2. Accountability Without Fear

   When accountability feels like punishment, people hide problems until they explode. System Trust ensures accountability is about solutions, not scapegoats.

   - *Question for CEOs: Do my teams call out issues early or wait until the fire is too big to contain?*

3. Cohesion That Withstands Conflict

   Great teams don't avoid tension—they leverage it. Cohesive teams can argue fiercely without breaking trust.

   - *Question for CEOs: Is my team avoiding tough conversations or engaging in productive conflict?*

4. Predictability Over Perfection

   Consistency beats brilliance in execution. A predictable system of decision-making, follow-ups, and learning loops creates high-trust environments.

   - *Question for CEOs: Does my leadership team know what to expect from me, or do they feel like they're navigating shifting goalposts?*

5. Speed of Repair, Not Just Speed of Action

    Execution breakdowns are inevitable. What sets great
    organizations apart is how fast they recognize and fix them.

    - *Question for CEOs: Do we learn from execution failures fast
      enough to prevent repeat mistakes?*

6. Leadership that Signals Safety

    People don't speak up when they feel their careers are at risk.
    Trust amplifiers ensure leaders create a space where honesty
    fuels execution, not fear.

    - *Question for CEOs: Do my teams challenge assumptions or
      play it safe to avoid rocking the boat?*

Why This Book? Why Now?

CEOs today are under unprecedented pressure:

- Shorter tenures—Boards get impatient if results don't come fast.

- Tougher stakeholder demands—Investors want growth; employees want meaning.

- Complex execution gaps—Brilliant strategies stall because teams operate in silos or play politics.

I spent the last decade researching why some organizations execute flawlessly while others choke under their own weight. I interviewed and surveyed 100+ CXOs across industries, analyzed execution patterns, and studied what separates 'brilliant ideas' from real-world success.

What I found was simple:

Execution isn't about hiring smarter people. It's about designing an environment where smart people can work together—without friction, fear, or politics.

My objective in writing this book is to create a playbook for CEOs and leaders who want to:

- ✔ Spot the execution traps that keep your strategy from taking off.

- ✔ Diagnose your leadership team—Is it a well-oiled machine or a Riot of Raptors?

✔ Fix accountability without crushing morale.

✔ Foster a culture where challenge is equal to growth, not a political landmine.

✔ Master the CEO's hardest job: Balancing results with relationships.

Because at the end of the day, your strategy is only as strong as your team's trust in each other, in you, and in the system you've built.

Acknowledgments

No journey—intellectual, professional, or personal—is ever walked alone. This book is a culmination of years of learning, reflecting, and engaging in deep conversations that shift perspectives and challenge long-held assumptions. As I put these thoughts into words, I am keenly aware of the countless people who have shaped my thinking, pushed my boundaries, and, at times, believed in my capacity more than I did.

To the leaders, colleagues, and mentors I have had the privilege of working with—thank you for your generosity in sharing your experiences, allowing me into the sacred spaces of your leadership dilemmas, and trusting me to capture your stories with depth and nuance. Each conversation has been a window into the unseen mechanics of leadership—the moments of doubt, courage, and conviction that define great teams and organizations.

A special thanks to the many leaders who participated in the surveys and conversations that shaped this book. Your willingness to engage, reflect, and share openly has provided invaluable insights into the nuances of leadership and team dynamics. This book would not exist without your candor, your stories, and your willingness to examine leadership beyond the surface.

To the leaders whose interviews shaped this book—your wisdom, and experiences have not only enriched my understanding but have illuminated the path for others who will read it. I am deeply grateful for the time, energy, and insights you so generously shared.

A special thanks to the leaders whose insights have been quoted in this book:

Mr. Aakash Moondhra – Co-Founder of India Secondary Fiduciaries, former Global CFO of PayU, and a leader in fintech and private equity, has played a pivotal role in scaling organizations. His insights on balancing accountability with cohesion and the importance of trust in leadership demonstrate the complexity of building high-performing teams.

Mr. Aditya Pande – Currently the Group CEO of InterGlobe Enterprises, Aditya has led high-growth businesses across multiple sectors. His reflections on navigating power dynamics, early intervention in leadership, and succession planning reveal the delicate balance between structure and adaptability.

Mr. C.P. Gurnani – Former CEO & MD of Tech Mahindra, CP transformed the company into a global IT powerhouse, leading its $6.5 billion growth journey. He is best known for orchestrating the landmark merger of Satyam Computers, a move that became a Harvard Business School case study on crisis management. His leadership philosophy of leading by example, making tough but fair decisions, and instilling a culture of continuous learning has left an indelible mark on the industry. His insights on resilience, strategic foresight, and people-centric leadership provide invaluable lessons on what it means to build a legacy.

Mr. Dhritiman Chakrabarti – A leader who has built his career spanning roles in business leadership, enterprise transformation, early-stage growth advisory & investing. From driving AI-led transformation at BRIDGEi2i Analytics to advising Fortune 500 companies on Enterprise Transformation at Korn Ferry, Willis Towers Watson & Aon, his expertise lies in working within complex environments across multiple geographies toward driving meaningful outcomes. His insights on the balance between consensus and decisiveness, performance clarity, and board engagement showcase the critical role that business leaders play in ensuring strategy turns into action.

Mr. Govind Shrikhande – Govind Shrikhande has spent decades transforming organizations by meticulously focusing on building trust, strengthening team dynamics, and ensuring strategy execution is not derailed by misalignment. From leading Shoppers Stop's turnaround to shaping governance practices across multiple industries, he has consistently demonstrated how a leader's ability to refine structures, behaviors, and culture can define an organization's success.

Mr. Himal Tewari – As the CHRO of Tata Power, Himal has navigated leadership across industries, bringing a deep understanding of how structural design impacts collaboration and execution. His reflections on how different industries shape team behavior highlight the importance of intentional leadership in fostering a collective spirit.

Mr. Himanshu Bahuguna – Leading India sales at Bank of America Merrill Lynch, Himanshu has mastered the balance between results and relationships. His perspectives on subcultures in large organizations, tenure-driven leadership styles, and crisis-driven trust-building provide a unique lens on high-performance teams.

Mr. Murli Ramachandran – Murli Ramachandran is a leader who has guided organizations through crisis and transformation, leveraging both strategic foresight and deep human insight. Whether at organizations or teams, which he has led or in his advisory roles, he has consistently balanced vision with execution, understanding that great leadership is not just about seeing the future but about mobilizing people to build it. His experiences underscore the power of resilience, instinct, and a well-calibrated balance between accountability and ambition.

Ms. Prabha Narasimhan – As the CEO of Colgate-Palmolive India, as well as in her previous roles, Prabha has steered teams through complex organizational landscapes, balancing structure with adaptability. Her expertise in leadership agility, overcoming systemic inertia, and fostering productive conflict provides valuable insights for leaders driving transformation and execution.

Mr. Prithvijit Roy – His journey spans from building a high-growth AI consulting startup to leading global AI and analytics strategy at a multinational firm, giving him an insider's view of how leadership dynamics shape execution success at different scales. He brings a rare perspective that blends deep expertise in corporate strategy, AI-driven decision-making, and entrepreneurial leadership. His ability to navigate both startup agility and corporate complexity has given him unique insights into how trust, alignment, and strategic clarity determine whether leadership teams thrive or fracture.

Mr. Sundararaman Ramamurthy – As MD & CEO of BSE, Sundar has played a key role in shaping financial governance and long-term institutional stability. His perspectives on ethical leadership, long-term thinking, and systemic resilience serve as a powerful guide for leaders who seek to build institutions that last.

To my teachers – those from my formative years and those at TISS and INSEAD—who instilled in me the joy of inquiry and the discipline of seeing beyond the obvious. A special thanks to Professor Michael Jarrett and Professor Erik Van der Loo, whose wisdom and guidance taught me the art of reflection and helped me understand that leadership is not just about results but about identity, relationships, and impact. To all my INSEAD teachers, who opened up new ways of thinking, forcing me to question what I thought I knew—you have helped shape not just my career but my way of seeing the world.

To my friends – those remarkable souls who have stood by me through seasons of doubt and discovery. You have trusted my journey, often more than I have, and reminded me time and again that I am capable of more than I believe. Your belief has been the wind beneath my wings.

To my parents and my brother, my unwavering constants—thank you for being my roots and my wings. You have given me the foundation of love and resilience, and the freedom to explore, question, and evolve. Without your grounding presence, none of this would have been possible.

To Roger, who showed me that I can and should reach for the stars.

To Mukti, whose wisdom and compassion helped me heal in ways I never thought possible, guiding me to finally fall in love with my life and, most importantly, with myself.

To my children – Siddharth and Aditi, my greatest teachers. Your intelligence, wisdom, and spirit illuminate my life in ways I never imagined. You remind me every day that learning is a lifelong pursuit, and that curiosity and courage walk hand in hand.

And finally, to my husband, Ravi – the person who sees me in my entirety. You have been my anchor and my rock, steadfast in your support, endlessly patient, and unwavering in your belief in me. Thank you for not just standing by my side but for actively shaping this book—reading through every chapter, challenging my arguments, and offering insights that sharpened my thinking. This book, in many ways, is a reflection of our conversations, your wisdom, and your quiet yet profound way of making me better.

To each of you – whether mentioned here or not—who have touched my life with your insights, friendship, guidance, and love, this book carries your imprint.

With deep gratitude,

Shweta

Methodology

The methodology for this study combines primary qualitative insights from interviews with senior leaders across various industries with secondary research into existing literature and case studies on strategy execution and team dynamics. This dual approach ensures a comprehensive understanding of the interplay between interpersonal relationships, trust within, and strategic outcomes within C-suite teams.

Data Collection

Primary Research

Insights from 100 CXOs

To deepen the understanding of the critical factors influencing strategy execution, I administered a comprehensive survey with 100 senior leaders and conducted interviews with many senior leaders across diverse industries. This mixed-method approach allowed me to capture both quantitative and qualitative insights, creating a rich foundation for analysis.

Participants

The survey engaged CEOs, managing directors, and other senior executives from sectors such as consulting, retail, aviation, manufacturing, financial services, energy, technology, healthcare, and consumer goods. These leaders, with extensive experience managing high-performing teams, provided a cross-sectional view of how various factors interplay in strategy execution.

Survey Scope and Objectives

Participants were asked to prioritize and assess key factors influencing strategy execution, including accountability, cohesion, decision-making, conflict resolution, and adaptability during crises. The responses helped to identify trends, priorities, and variances across industries, revealing the underlying dynamics that drive success or lead to stagnation.

Interview Methodology

To supplement the survey findings, semi-structured interviews were conducted with a subset of these leaders. This format offered guided inquiry while allowing flexibility for open-ended discussions. Participants shared personal anecdotes, challenges, and strategies that illuminated the realities of leadership, team dynamics, and execution barriers.

Format and Duration

The interviews, lasting between 45-60 minutes, were conducted through a mix of in-person meetings and video conferencing, ensuring accessibility for participants worldwide. This dual format maintained the depth and authenticity of the discussions while accommodating logistical needs.

Key Takeaways

The dual approach of surveys and interviews provided a nuanced understanding of the factors that leaders perceive as critical for strategy execution. Insights gained from this research form the backbone of the book, offering actionable strategies grounded in real-world experiences and evidence.

Secondary Research

- **Literature Review:** Relevant academic and industry research on strategy execution, leadership behaviors, and organizational dynamics was analyzed. Studies from leading sources such as Harvard Business Review, McKinsey reports, and case studies from high-performing organizations were incorporated to contextualize and validate findings.

- **Case Studies:** Examination of specific organizational success and failure cases provided additional insights into the factors influencing strategy execution. These include companies from varied sectors, such as technology giants, innovative startups, and legacy organizations navigating transformation.

Analytical Framework

1. **Thematic Analysis:** The primary and secondary data were coded and categorized to identify recurring patterns, unique insights, and contextual nuances. Themes such as 'synergistic superstars', 'riot of raptors', and 'cocoon of connections' emerged, offering a structured framework for categorizing team dynamics and their impact on strategy execution.

2. **Archetypal Categorization:** To preserve anonymity while providing relatable narratives, participant insights are presented using archetype names. These archetypes encapsulate the essence of each leader's organizational experience, making the findings both vivid and accessible. So, names like The Architect, The Challenger, The Sage, etc., have been used throughout the book to preserve the anonymity of the interviewees.

Ethical Considerations

- **Confidentiality:** All participants were assured of their anonymity, with identifying information and sensitive details carefully anonymized.

- **Consent:** Explicit consent was obtained from all participants, with opportunities to review and refine interpretations of their input before publication.

I hope that by integrating insights from senior leaders across industries and anchoring these findings in robust secondary research, readers will gain a rich, multidimensional understanding of the dynamics influencing strategy execution. Throughout the text, readers will encounter anonymized archetypes and cross-industry examples, bringing to life the pivotal intersections of leadership, culture, and performance.

CHAPTER 1

The Uncomfortable Truth

"Trust is like oxygen. You don't notice it until it's running out."

-Barry, former CEO of a Fortune 500 company

Why Great Strategies Fail

A CXO I interviewed shared a story that stuck with me.

He had led two companies with identical strategies and equally talented teams. One thrived: *"It was like a symphony. We anticipated each other's moves, solved problems before they escalated, and operated with an unspoken rhythm of trust."*

The other? *"It was chaos. Every individual was brilliant, but together, it was like watching a dance troupe perform to completely different music."*

Both had the same strategy, but one had System Trust, and the other didn't. That was the difference between success and failure.

The Trust Paradox

70% of strategies fail—not because they're bad strategies but because organizations lack the trust to execute them. CEOs often mistake trust for a soft factor, but it is the invisible scaffolding that holds execution together. Without it:

- 45% of employees withhold critical information.

- 68% avoid raising concerns.

- Productivity drops by 50%.

Without trust, execution becomes a negotiation, not a flow. Every decision takes longer, every risk is avoided, and every failure is buried.

Yet, while 93% of CEOs recognize trust as critical, only 7% actively work on it. Why? Because trust is intangible—until it's gone.

System Trust: The CEO's Execution Advantage

High-trust companies outperform their peers significantly, in total shareholder return. Neuroscience confirms why: When people feel trusted, their brains release oxytocin, increasing cognitive function by 50%, reducing stress by 74%, and doubling energy levels.

Trust is not just about relationships; it's about systems. It is the difference between an organization that moves seamlessly and one that gets stuck in silos, bureaucracy, and second-guessing.

Execution thrives not on blind trust but engineered trust—where clarity, accountability, and psychological safety allow people to challenge assumptions, take ownership, and act decisively.

The CEO's Hardest Balancing Act

Every CEO faces a brutal truth:

You must deliver results while building trust—but most leadership teams don't inherit perfect systems, and time is never on your side.

The pressure to perform forces leaders to focus on accountability, but when trust is missing, accountability turns into fear, finger-pointing, and risk aversion.

The challenge isn't just creating great strategies—it's creating the trust infrastructure that allows them to succeed.

The Path Forward

If trust is the air your strategy breathes, it cannot be left to chance. CEOs must engineer trust into the very fabric of execution.

In the next chapters, we'll dive into the System Trust Matrix—a blueprint for diagnosing and building trust at scale. Because strategy alone doesn't drive results—System Trust does.

CHAPTER 2

Trust's Hidden Architecture: The Three Forces

"Great teams don't just happen. They're built on purpose, over time."

-The Harmonizer, CXO at a global financial institution

Why Do Some Teams Execute Flawlessly While Others Stall

Trusted companies can outperform their peers by up to 400% in terms of business outcomes. This performance boost is reflected in customer behavior, with 88% of customers who trust a brand being more likely to make repeat purchases.

The impact of trust extends to employee behavior and organizational culture. In high-trust environments, 79% of employees report being more motivated to work and less likely to leave their jobs. Conversely, productivity can suffer significantly in low-trust organizations, though the exact percentage drop would require further verification.

Yet, despite 93% of CEOs recognizing trust as critical, only 7% actively work on it.

Why? Because trust isn't a vague concept—it's an infrastructure powered by three invisible forces. These forces act like an organizational current—either accelerating execution or creating silent resistance.

The Three Forces of System Trust:

The 3 Forces of
System Trust

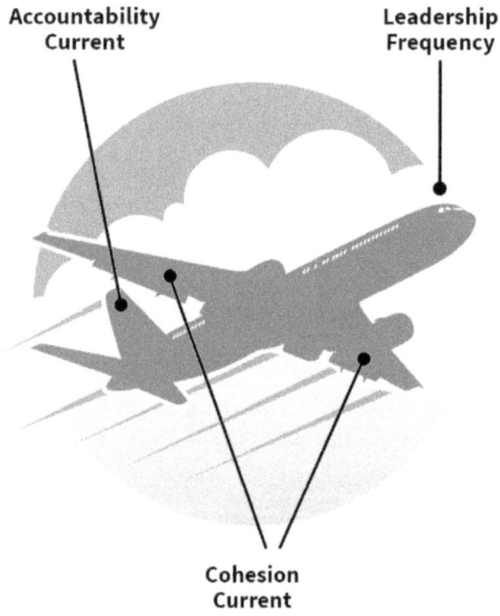

1. **The Accountability Current** – Does ownership flow naturally, or is it avoided?

2. **The Cohesion Current** – Do teams work as a unit and have each other's backs, or do they operate in silos?

3. **The Leadership Frequency** – Do leaders create clarity, or do they create confusion?

These forces don't operate in isolation—they interact, amplify, and shape an organization's ability to execute. Let's break them down.

1. The Accountability Current: Ownership vs. Evasion

When trust flows, accountability follows.

At a global fintech firm, The Architect observed that when trust was given upfront, accountability became a natural response—not an enforced demand. Problems were solved before they escalated, and feedback was a tool for growth, not blame.

In high-accountability cultures:

- People own their work—problems don't sit untouched in endless meetings.

- Decisions happen fast—there's no fear of stepping up.

- Feedback is constant and constructive—not a once-a-year formality.

Contrast that with organizations where accountability breaks down:

- Problems linger until they explode.

- More time is spent justifying inaction than taking action.

- Success is claimed by the loudest, while failures are blamed on the weakest.

The Refiner, a leader in retail, described his experience:

"I inherited a team where most of the time was spent defending why things didn't get done—rather than actually doing them. The lack of ownership was in the air."

Accountability is not a metric—it's an energy. Walk into a shop or office, and you can feel whether people are taking ownership—or avoiding responsibility. The question for leaders is:

Is accountability alive in your organization, or is it being buried under bureaucracy?

2. The Cohesion Current: Trust vs. Turf Wars

Cohesion isn't about team lunches or trust falls. It's about one simple question:

"Do people in this organization have each other's backs?"

High-cohesion teams argue fiercely but stay committed. They challenge each other but never let personal differences derail execution.

Cohesion in action:

- Information flows freely—not hoarded as political currency.

- Tension is productive—disagreements sharpen execution, not sabotage it.

- Success is shared—not used as leverage for personal gain.

Contrast that with low-cohesion teams:

- Decisions feel like tugs-of-war, with people pulling in different directions.

- Trust is transactional—people cover themselves before they cover the company.

- Failures result in finger-pointing, not learning.

One CEO admitted:

"It's heartbreaking, but many of my leaders wouldn't hesitate to throw their colleagues under the bus if it meant saving themselves."

You can see cohesion—or the lack of it—everywhere. In a high-trust restaurant, waiters instinctively cover for each other during peak hours. In a fractured one, they bicker, blame, and let customers suffer.

Is your team a unit—or a battlefield?

3. The Leadership Frequency: Command vs. Consult

Leadership isn't a style—it's a frequency. The best leaders know when to command with clarity and when to consult with curiosity.

In high-trust organizations:

- Leaders provide direction when needed but step back to let teams own execution.

- Employees feel both supported and empowered.

- Decision-making balances speed with inclusivity.

When leadership goes out of tune, two things happen:

1. **Over-Commanding Leaders:** They micromanage every decision, stifling ownership and initiative.

2. **Over-Consulting Leaders:** They avoid taking charge, leaving teams directionless and frustrated.

As *the Sage,* a turnaround leader in life sciences, put it:

"The strongest leadership signal isn't always about being the loudest. It's about knowing when to amplify others' voices—and when to cut through the noise with clarity."

The structure of the organization can also add or stifle this. As The Strategist put it, *"The structure of an organization can either make collaboration second nature or make it feel like a Herculean task. Leaders need to diagnose this early and act deliberately."*

Great leaders modulate their frequency:

- In crisis? Command with clarity.

- In growth? Create space for collaboration.

Are you leading at the right frequency, or is your leadership creating static?

The Three Forces that Shape Trust:

Like the warp and weft of a master weaver's loom, three forces shape every organization's reality.

The Accountability Current: Accountability current focuses on accountability as perceived in the system. Think of accountability not as a metric but as an electrical current flowing through your organization. In Mumbai's bustling wholesale vegetable markets, traders don't need KPIs—accountability flows naturally because every action directly affects survival. As the Architect discovered at the global FinTech organization, *"When trust is given upfront, accountability becomes a natural response, not an enforced demand."*

When the focus on accountability is good, and the organization buzzes with the energy of everyone taking accountability, problems resolve themselves long before they gather enough weight to become meetings.

Here, a culture of proactive ownership ensures that small issues are addressed at their roots, sparing everyone from the expense of unproductive escalation. Feedback flows faster than office gossip, creating a buzz not of rumors but of continuous learning. Success and failure, too, find clear addresses—everyone knows where credit is due and where accountability lies. It's a system that thrives on clarity, speed, and trust.

In my interview with the Mentor, he says, *"Focus on accountability, as if it is a sacred object and no one would risk dropping something that feels so sacred."*

In contrast, when the accountability charge falters in an organization, a very different story emerges. Problems are left to sit and age, not gracefully but expensively, ignored until they become impossible to manage. Instead of being the connective tissue that strengthens relationships, feedback gets lost in the shuffle—diluted and misinterpreted. And success and failure? They drift, perpetually homeless, with no one claiming responsibility or learning from their lessons. It's an environment where ambiguity reigns, and progress gets tangled in its own inertia.

The Refiner talks about his experience in the retail industry and says that when he inherited the team, the largest amount of time was spent defending why things didn't get done rather than actually doing them. He says, *"The lack of ownership was in the air."*

You can feel the accountability current when you enter an organization—or even a shop. You can feel the energy that hums through the place, telling you whether problems are handled with care or left to fester.

When I walk into a client's office, a shop, or a restaurant, I notice the small and big ways the accountability current buzzes—or falters. In high-current places, accountability is alive and electric. A shopkeeper notices a customer looking confused and steps in with, "How can I help you find what you're looking for?" before they even have to ask. In a well-run restaurant, an empty water glass is refilled without a word, and if a dish doesn't meet the standard, the waiter immediately acknowledges it, saying, "Let me take care of this for you." These are the hallmarks of an environment where ownership is woven into the culture.

Low-current places, by contrast, feel stagnant. Walk into a poorly run shop, and you might stand around waiting while employees chat with each other, oblivious to your presence. At a struggling restaurant, your waiter avoids eye contact when your meal takes too long, or worse, blames the kitchen when you finally complain.

Accountability currents are cultural. You can feel them in the air. High currents inspire confidence and pride, from the corner cubicle to the executive suite, from the stockroom to the shop floor. Low currents, by contrast, sap energy and create a culture of evasion and defensiveness.

The question for leaders is simple: What kind of current is running through your organization? Are you willing to do the work to make it buzz?

The Cohesion Current:

Cohesion is about focusing on relationships and intrateam trust. It is the feeling that people have when they feel, others have their backs. Cohesion isn't about team lunches or trust falls. It's the gravitational field that determines whether people orbit together or spiral apart.

Cohesion centers on relationships and intrateam trust—the deep-rooted belief that others will always have your back. It isn't about team lunches or trust falls. Instead, it's the gravitational force that determines whether people orbit together in alignment or spiral apart into dysfunction. As the Adaptive Navigator observed, *"The more you increase task conflict, relationship conflict actually goes down"*—a counterintuitive insight that challenges conventional wisdom about team harmony.

Cohesion is not defined by polite conversations or the absence of conflict. On the contrary, cohesive teams argue passionately, disagree openly, and challenge one another frequently—all in the pursuit of excellence. Yet above all, these teams hold sacred the value: *"I may disagree with you, even be disappointed in you, but I will always have your back."* This principle creates a foundation of unwavering trust, even in the face of disagreements.

When cohesion is strong, an organization hums with the rhythm of collaboration. Information flows like water in a clear stream—unobstructed, refreshing, and nourishing every part of the system it touches. In this environment, conflicts sharpen ideas rather than knives, fostering a space where diverse perspectives are embraced and leveraged for innovation. Success becomes a shared feast, with every member of the team pulling up a chair to celebrate their contributions. It's a culture of interdependence, where no one eats alone, and collective effort consistently outpaces individual genius.

As the Strategist puts it, *"Cohesion feels like being part of a beautifully choreographed orchestra—each section playing its part in harmony, amplifying the whole."*

In contrast, when the cohesion current weakens, the organization devolves into silos and suspicion. Information moves like gold in a thieves' market—hoarded, traded with mistrust, and never freely shared. Conflicts become either buried in uncomfortable silence or explode into nuclear fallout, damaging relationships and creating scars that linger long after the initial issue has passed. Success becomes a lonely summit, scaled by individuals who stand at the top with no one to share the view and no team to sustain the climb.

I see this many times in organizations. One of my clients said in a moment of candor, *"It's heartbreaking for me to admit this, but many of my team members won't hesitate to throw the others under the bus without a moment of consideration."*

The Challenger described such an environment: *"It's like being stuck in a tug-of-war where everyone is pulling in different directions, and the rope frays before anyone makes progress."*

You can sense the cohesion current when you step into an organization—or even a shop or restaurant. In high-cohesion spaces, it shows up in the seamless teamwork of the staff. In a shop, a cashier might call out to a floor assistant to help a confused customer, and the assistant responds immediately, guiding them with genuine care. You notice how smoothly the team communicates—there's no territoriality, no "that's not my department." In a restaurant, you see the waitstaff effortlessly coordinating with the kitchen and each other. One server notices that another's table is running low on water and steps in to refill glasses without hesitation or resentment. Everyone's focus is on the customer's experience, not their own turf.

By contrast, in a low-cohesion setting, the cracks are visible even to outsiders. In a shop, a customer might stand waiting for help while staff members argue about whose job it is. Questions are met with shrugs or defensiveness, and the energy feels disjointed. In a restaurant, you might see servers bickering quietly or a manager stepping in to patch up issues that should have been resolved among the team. If something goes wrong—an incorrect order or a missing item—the blame game starts, and the customer is left in the crossfire of poor collaboration.

Cohesion currents are deeply cultural. High-field strength inspires trust, collaboration, and collective pride that binds teams together. Low-field strength, however, breeds isolation, mistrust, and a focus on self-preservation.

> **The question for leaders is this: Is the cohesion current in your organization a lifeline or a liability? And what steps are you taking to ensure it flows freely and with strength?**

The Leadership Command vs. Consult Resonance

Leadership isn't a style; it's a frequency. The best leaders modulate between directive and democratic modes like a skilled radio operator, tuning into the specific needs of their team and environment.

Sometimes the situation demands a commanding presence—a clear, decisive voice cutting through the noise and guiding the team with certainty. At other times, the consultative mode is key, creating space for others to contribute, collaborate, and innovate. Great leaders don't pick a lane; they adapt, shifting between these modes with finesse.

As the Sage shared during the turnaround of a life sciences company, *"The strongest signal often comes from knowing when to amplify others' voices."* During a critical turnaround phase, the Sage called on their team to speak up, drawing on their expertise to uncover bottlenecks and craft solutions. But in moments of crisis—when decisions needed to be swift and unambiguous— their voice became the anchor, cutting through uncertainty and aligning the organization on a singular course.

When leaders strike the right resonance, the organization thrives. Command and consult exist in a harmonious rhythm. Teams feel both supported and empowered, knowing their leader will step in with clarity when the stakes are high yet step back to allow creativity and ownership to flourish. This balance builds trust, resilience, and agility.

In contrast, when leadership resonance is off, the results are palpable. A leader stuck in command mode can stifle initiative, leaving the team feeling over-managed and undervalued. The air becomes heavy with compliance rather than commitment. On the flip side, a leader perpetually consulting without providing direction risks creating a vacuum where ambiguity breeds frustration and decisions are endlessly delayed. The organization feels adrift, lacking the grounding of decisive leadership.

You can sense this leadership frequency even in a shop or restaurant. In high-resonance environments, a shop manager might step in during a busy rush to reorganize checkout lines or quickly resolve a customer complaint, ensuring smooth operations. At the same time, they'll pull their team aside after the rush, asking for ideas on how to improve future workflows. Similarly, in a well-run restaurant, a manager might step into the kitchen during a sudden rush to reassign tasks or ensure orders are expedited while simultaneously gathering input from the staff afterward to refine processes.

By contrast, low-resonance leadership is immediately noticeable. In a shop, the manager might bark orders to employees without listening to their challenges, creating tension and resentment among the staff. Or, on the flip side, they might leave employees to manage a chaotic situation with no clear direction, resulting in frazzled staff and frustrated customers. In a struggling restaurant, you might see a manager hesitating to step in when the kitchen falls behind or pushing blame onto servers during a customer complaint, leaving the team disorganized and demoralized.

Leadership resonance is a dance, not a doctrine. It requires constant calibration, like tuning an instrument to match the song.

The question for leaders is this: Are you playing in harmony with your team, or are you stuck on a single note? And how will you ensure your leadership frequency brings out the best in those you lead?

As we bring together the dimensions of Leadership Style, Focus on Accountability, and Focus on Cohesion, it becomes clear that these forces don't act in isolation—they converge to create the unique dynamics of any team. They shape how trust is built, how strategies are executed, and how teams navigate challenges. But how do these elements interact to define a team's identity and performance? In the next chapter, we will explore the System Trust Matrix, a powerful framework that maps these dynamics into four distinct quadrants, each with its own trust signature. This lens will not only reveal where your team currently stands but also provide a pathway for transformation.

5 Key Takeaways

1. Trust isn't abstract—it's built through three organizational forces. Accountability, cohesion, and leadership frequency determine whether trust fuels execution or creates friction.

2. Accountability must flow naturally, not be enforced. High-accountability cultures solve problems before they escalate, while low-accountability cultures bury issues until they explode.

3. Cohesion isn't about harmony—it's about trust in action. High-cohesion teams challenge each other without breaking trust, while low-cohesion teams operate in silos, hoarding information and avoiding ownership.

4. Leadership is about tuning into the right frequency. Great leaders know when to command with clarity and when to consult with curiosity. One-dimensional leadership creates bottlenecks.

5. Your strategy's success depends on the strength of these forces. If accountability, cohesion, and leadership clarity are strong, execution happens seamlessly. If anyone is weak, strategy stalls.

3 Questions Every CEO Must Ask

💡 What kind of accountability current runs through my organization? Do people own problems, or do they avoid them until they become crises?

💡 Is my team operating as a unit—or are they pulling in different directions? Do people share information freely, or is trust being eroded by politics and silos?

💡 Am I leading at the right frequency? Do I provide clarity when needed and step back when it's time for others to take ownership? Or am I stuck in a leadership style that isn't serving execution?

CHAPTER 3

The System Trust Matrix— Mapping the Execution Gap

*"Trust isn't just a leadership philosophy—it's
a strategic advantage."*

Despite its abstract nature, trust creates predictable patterns in organizations. It determines whether execution flows or stalls, whether people collaborate or compete, and whether strategy translates into results or dies in silos.

Through my research, I've identified four distinct organizational trust states—quadrants that emerge based on how accountability and cohesion interact. Together, they form the System Trust Matrix, a framework that allows leaders to diagnose trust breakdowns, course-correct team behaviors, and optimize execution.

Every leadership team falls into one of these four quadrants— and each comes with a trust signature that shapes performance, culture, and long-term viability.

Understanding where your leadership team operates is the first step to engineering the trust infrastructure needed for strategy execution. Let's break these quadrants down.

The 4 quadrants of System Trust Matrix

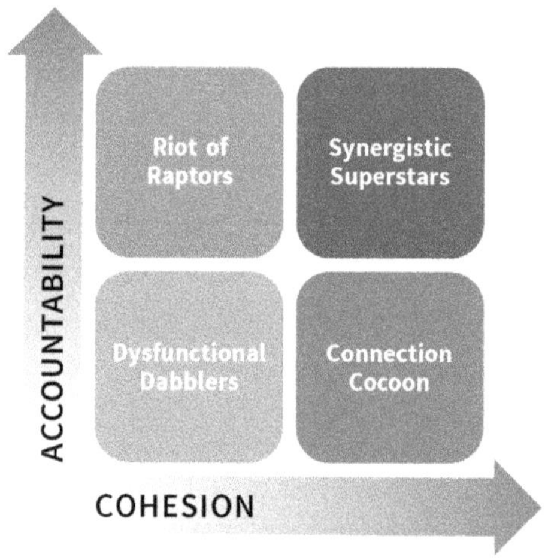

QUADRANT 1:

Synergistic Superstars - The Trust Signature of Empowered Unity: Where high accountability meets high cohesion, creating organizational superfluidity. Synergistic reflects the idea that the whole becomes far greater than the sum of its parts—where individual strengths combine seamlessly to produce results that no single person could achieve alone. Superstars speak to the excellence that emerges, not as isolated brilliance but as a collective force driving the team toward extraordinary outcomes.

In this space, we see the magic of teams that don't just function—they flourish, powered by their shared commitment to high standards and unshakable bonds of trust. Any leader's ultimate goal is to create an environment where collaboration and accountability feed into each other, lifting the entire organization to new heights.

The workplace flows with an almost magical ease, where people operate in sync, barriers dissolve, and productivity feels effortless. This is what I call organizational superfluidity. It's a place where leadership, both directive and democratic, weaves together seamlessly, amplifying strengths and smoothing over friction. In this quadrant, trust is a force multiplier.

When directive leadership takes the reins, it sets the foundation. Clear performance guardrails are established, but they feel more like springboards than prison walls—guiding the team with clarity while giving them the freedom to excel. For instance, in a high-performing retail chain, a store manager might set unambiguous sales targets and customer service metrics, ensuring that every team member knows exactly what success looks like. Yet, these standards are not a source of fear. Instead, they inspire the team to reach higher, creating a shared sense of pride in exceeding expectations.

Directive leaders also know when to step in with swift, decisive interventions. Imagine a restaurant where a sudden influx of customers threatens to overwhelm the kitchen. A skilled manager immediately reorganizes tasks, redistributing the workload with precision. Far from resenting the interruption, the team welcomes it as a necessary course correction, allowing them to recover smoothly and keep delivering top-notch service. In these environments, high standards are not a source of dread but a shared commitment that inspires everyone to do their best. To put it in the words of the Mentor: *"Ethics over competence, every time. Execution works best when trust and discipline coexist."*

Directive leadership establishes trust through structure, where clear systems and transparent decision-making create psychological safety. Teams trust the system to evaluate and reward performance fairly. Cross-functional collaboration is seamless, and mistakes are viewed as opportunities for learning rather than failures. Imagine a technology company where teams align tightly to well-defined OKRs (Objectives and Key Results), but leaders also foster open feedback loops, ensuring employees feel supported and valued.

On the other hand, democratic leadership activates the team's untapped potential. Organic problem-solving networks emerge, springing into action before issues even have a chance to escalate. In a shop, for example, team members might take the initiative to reorganize stock when they notice a bottleneck at the counter—without needing to be told. This kind of ownership and collaboration is fueled by a culture of psychological safety, where employees feel free to take calculated risks and innovate.

Democratic leadership also nurtures cross-functional collaboration that feels as natural as breathing. Picture a tech startup where engineers, marketers, and designers regularly meet to brainstorm ideas. Instead of territorial battles, there's a fluid exchange of insights, with everyone focused on solving the same problem rather than protecting their domain. This kind of synergy not only prevents friction but turns diversity into a competitive advantage.

Democratic leadership builds trust through empowerment, enabling individuals to innovate and take ownership. Teams trust each other's judgment and feel safe experimenting, knowing that collaboration will lead to collective wisdom. Symptoms of this trust include an open, buzzing workplace culture where ideas flow freely, and conflicts, when they arise, are resolved constructively. For example, a retail brand with an empowered frontline staff might respond to customer feedback in real time, improving both customer experience and operational efficiency.

Together, directive and democratic leadership create a dynamic equilibrium. The former provides structure and clarity, while the latter fosters creativity and connection. In environments like this, teams move with both precision and agility, proving that leadership isn't about choosing one style over another—it's about blending them to create a culture where both accountability and cohesion thrive. The result? An organization where success isn't just a goal—it's a way of life.

A great example of Synergistic Superstars in action can be drawn from cricket, particularly the legendary Indian cricket team under M.S. Dhoni's captaincy. Known for his calm demeanor and sharp strategic mind, Dhoni built a team where accountability and cohesion worked hand in hand, creating a powerhouse that dominated various formats of the game.

Directive Leadership in Action:

Dhoni's leadership was decisive when the stakes were high. Take the 2011 Cricket World Cup final. Chasing a challenging target against Sri Lanka, Dhoni embraced Tendulkar's advice, elevating himself in the batting order ahead of an in-form Yuvraj Singh. This wasn't just a tactical move—it was a clear statement of accountability. His unbeaten 91 runs not only secured the win but also demonstrated that he wasn't afraid to shoulder the responsibility when it mattered most. His swift, decisive interventions under pressure created a culture where high standards were expected and met without fear.

Democratic Leadership in Action:

At the same time, Dhoni was known for empowering his players and nurturing a sense of ownership and collaboration within the team. He famously encouraged young players like Virat Kohli and Ravichandran Ashwin to express themselves freely, fostering innovation and adaptability on the field. His ability to create a psychologically safe environment allowed players to take risks without fearing harsh criticism.

Synergy in Motion:

The hallmark of this team's success was its ability to operate as a cohesive unit. Each player knew their role and trusted their teammates to perform theirs. Whether it was Zaheer Khan delivering crucial breakthroughs with the ball, Yuvraj Singh dominating with both bat and ball, or Sachin Tendulkar anchoring innings with precision, the team worked like a finely tuned orchestra. When the pressure was highest, such as in knockout matches, they came together with an unspoken understanding, turning individual brilliance into collective triumph.

This combination of Dhoni's directive clarity and democratic empowerment created a team that thrived under pressure and set benchmarks of excellence. It became an example of what happens when accountability meets cohesion. It's why they weren't just a great cricket team—they were Synergistic Superstars.

3 Key Takeaways from Synergistic Superstars

1. **Great execution thrives on a balance between structure and empowerment.**

   High-performing teams aren't just disciplined; they are also adaptive. Directive leadership provides clear goals and accountability, while democratic leadership fosters ownership, innovation, and cross-functional trust.

2. **Trust acts as a force multiplier when accountability and cohesion reinforce each other.**

   When teams trust the system, they operate with confidence, make decisions faster, and solve problems proactively—without fear of blame. This creates organizational superfluidity, where execution happens seamlessly.

3. **High-trust teams outperform because they combine individual excellence with collective synergy.**

   Like M.S. Dhoni's leadership, the best organizations blend decisiveness with empowerment, ensuring that people take responsibility while feeling psychologically safe to innovate and challenge the status quo.

Reflection Question for CEOs:

💡 *Is my leadership team structured in a way that balances clear accountability with trust-driven empowerment, allowing both high performance and high collaboration to thrive?*

QUADRANT 2:

Riot of Raptors - The Trust Signature of Fragmented Competition: This is the space with a very high focus on accountability but low cohesion—like a particle accelerator without containment. I call it the Riot of Raptors because it vividly captures the chaotic energy of an organization where accountability runs high, but cohesion is painfully absent.

Watching raptors in the sky—falcons, hawks, or eagles—it's clear they are powerful, agile, and fiercely independent. But when a group of them appears together, you do see not harmony but a chaotic scramble. Each bird dives, swoops, and jostles for dominance, hunting the same prey with no coordination or shared strategy. They're breathtakingly capable as individuals, but together, their energy collides and cancels out, creating an impression of disorder rather than strength.

In organizations that embody this dynamic, the same raw power and potential are present, but instead of working as a team, individuals prioritize their own goals. Accountability is high, but cohesion is low, leaving the collective power of the group untapped and often, self-destructive. It's a spectacle of brilliance wasted on disarray, with too many talons reaching for the same prize and none of them securing it effectively.

The result? Frenzied activity that burns bright in the short term but may self-destruct in the long term, with individual brilliance overshadowing collective progress.

In a Riot of Raptors, directive leadership may turn into a double-edged sword. The hyper-focus on metrics and results can quickly transform colleagues into competitors.

In this space, trust may seem transactional. Teams trust systems—such as metrics and dashboards—more than they trust each other. Collaboration happens only when formally mandated and information is treated as a competitive advantage rather than a shared resource. This creates a 'Hunger Games' environment where individuals and departments operate as competitors, not collaborators. Symptoms include spectacular short-term results but high team fatigue, turnover, and innovation bottlenecks. For example, in high-pressure sales teams, colleagues may prioritize personal targets over team success, eroding long-term organizational cohesion.

For example, consider high-stakes sales teams in certain Indian corporate sectors, like telecom or real estate. In one well-known case, sales managers at a leading Indian real estate firm were pitted against each other with intense targets, leading to cutthroat tactics. While individual performers achieved remarkable numbers, there was no cross-sharing of strategies, and no collaboration to improve overall sales efficiency. Over time, this hyper-competitive environment eroded trust and morale, turning a team of potential superstars into isolated islands.

Directive leadership in these environments also manifests as a command-and-control style that stifles collaboration. Take the infamous collapse of Kingfisher Airlines, which was partly attributed to a top-down, authoritarian leadership approach. High accountability was demanded of employees, but decisions were tightly centralized. Employees were left scrambling to meet impossible expectations without clear communication or support, and as financial pressures mounted, silos deepened, and the organization spiraled into dysfunction. The intense achievement pressure created individual stars—pilots, cabin crew, and sales leaders who excelled in their lanes—but left the broader system fractured, unable to hold itself together.

Meanwhile, democratic leadership struggles to take root in a Riot of Raptors. Under democratic leadership, competitive trust emerges, with teams forming small trust islands that often compete with each other. Without a unified direction, innovation becomes fragmented, with knowledge sharing limited to tightly knit clusters. Symptoms include siloed initiatives, parallel efforts, and fragmented strategic focus. Think of organizations where regional offices or departments pursue conflicting goals, leading to inefficiencies and diluted impact. Trust deficits within the team make consensus-building an exercise in futility, like herding velociraptors—fast, unpredictable, and dangerously self-interested.

Attempts at collaboration often get weaponized into political games. An example can be found in certain Indian political coalitions where high-profile alliances have faltered due to internal power struggles. Each party or leader fights to secure their turf, often prioritizing their agendas over the coalition's broader goals. The result? Stagnation, infighting, and a failure to deliver on collective promises.

Even when team autonomy exists, it frequently leads to competing fiefdoms instead of synergy. Consider cricket again, specifically the Indian team in the early 2000s before the leadership of Sourav Ganguly. Back then, the team was filled with incredible talent—stars like Sachin Tendulkar, Rahul Dravid, and Anil Kumble—but lacked cohesion. Players often focused on individual performances, and there was little sense of a unified direction or camaraderie. This mindset hampered the team's ability to win crucial matches. It wasn't until Ganguly's leadership emphasized collective goals and mutual trust that the team began to thrive as a cohesive unit.

In this space, the focus on accountability without cohesion breeds a paradox. On the surface, it appears as though everyone is working harder than ever, yet progress feels elusive. The energy of high accountability is misdirected, creating a churn of activity with little alignment. Without containment, this high-energy environment doesn't just fail to thrive—it risks tearing itself apart.

As the Sage put it, *"Crisis can temporarily create high accountability; but if trust is missing, once the crisis is over, execution collapses into dysfunction."* The Refiner echoed this when he spoke about his endeavor to build a very trusted retail brand: *"Trust isn't given; it's earned through transparency, fairness, and accountability. In high-accountability but low-trust environments, unresolved tensions sink execution."*

Impact on Execution: Teams focus on performance at all costs, leading to short-term success but long-term fractures. Execution is fragmented, and strategy collapses in cross-functional misalignment.

The challenge for leaders in this setting is immense but not insurmountable. The Legacy Builder stated that it is not impossible to build a healthy culture no matter where one is at. However, one needs to confront the behaviors early on. *"If you let toxic behaviors linger, you're endorsing them."*

The question becomes: How do you transform a Riot of Raptors into a harmonious force where accountability is tempered with trust and cohesion? And do you have the courage to confront the deep fractures in the system before they devour the organization whole?

3 Key Takeaways from Riot of Raptors

1. **High accountability without trust leads to internal competition, not collaboration.**

   Teams in this quadrant focus on individual success over collective achievement, creating silos, friction, and execution bottlenecks. Trust is transactional rather than relational, making alignment difficult.

2. **Short-term performance can make long-term dysfunction.**

   These organizations often deliver spectacular results early on but at the cost of burnout, high turnover, and unsustainable execution. Over time, a lack of cohesion weakens resilience, innovation, and adaptability.

3. **Without intervention, Riot of Raptors cultures self-destruction.**

   Toxic competition, political maneuvering, and lack of trust in leadership create a high-energy but unstable environment. To fix this, leaders must actively foster cross-team trust, reward collaboration, and dismantle silos.

   Reflection Question for CEOs:

   💡 *Am I incentivizing individual performance at the cost of team cohesion, creating a culture where competition undermines execution?*

QUADRANT 3:

Connection Cocoon - The Trust Signature of Comfort without Growth: High cohesion but low accountability is comfortable but ultimately unsustainable. I call it the Connection Cocoon because it captures the warm yet suffocating dynamic of a space where cohesion is high but accountability is painfully low. Imagine a cozy cocoon where everyone feels safe, supported, and united—but no one dares to emerge and fly. It's a place of deep connection and comfort but also stagnation. Progress slows, hard truths are avoided, and tough decisions are postponed indefinitely. What begins as harmony eventually becomes complacency, leaving the team ill-equipped to face challenges or deliver results.

The Comfort Trap often undermines directive leadership, turning decisive action into a minefield. In this space, directive leadership fosters comfort-based trust. Teams value interpersonal bonds over systems, creating an environment where harmony takes precedence over performance. Feedback is softened to maintain relationships, and accountability is avoided for fear of disrupting the peace. Symptoms include stagnation, missed opportunities for innovation, and an insular culture that views external challenges as the enemy. For example, in family businesses where relationships outweigh results, underperforming team members might be shielded from accountability, ultimately dragging the organization down.

Leaders find themselves holding back from hard conversations for fear of disrupting the group's harmony. Performance issues are swept under the rug, hidden behind shields of personal relationships and camaraderie. Goals are watered down into vague suggestions, softened to avoid upsetting the peace. It's like walking on eggshells in a house where no one wants to hurt anyone's feelings—except the cracks keep growing underfoot.

Democratic leadership, in this context, becomes an escape hatch from accountability. It's easy to frame every decision as a group effort, using collaboration as a shield against conflict or change. Teams spend more time maintaining their comfort zone than confronting their blind spots. The warmth of relationships masks underperformance, as meetings become endless loops of consensus-seeking rather than action. Everyone gets along, but nothing meaningful gets done.

With democratic leadership, trust shifts to social trust, where the team prioritizes community and consensus over mission and effectiveness. Decision-making becomes slow and diffused, with accountability seen as a threat to harmony. Symptoms include endless discussions, avoidance of necessary conflict, and performance conversations that lack substance. Picture an organization where everyone is deeply connected, but hard decisions are continually deferred, causing operational inefficiencies and misalignment with strategic goals.

As the Lead-By-Example Leader warns, *"It's like a family business where everyone's too nice to tell Uncle Joe he's not cutting it anymore. Love without standards isn't really love at all."*

An example of this dynamic can be seen in certain legacy organizations or even tight-knit startup teams. In one well-known case, a multi-generational family-run business in India faltered because no one wanted to challenge the senior leadership's outdated strategies. The company prided itself on its family culture, but the reluctance to introduce fresh accountability allowed inefficiency to spread unchecked. Harmony was preserved but at the cost of performance and, eventually, profitability.

In Connection Cocoon, this dynamic is also visible in teams that avoid conflict even when it's sorely needed. Consider a small hospitality business where the staff shares a wonderful camaraderie. The front desk manager is beloved but chronically disorganized, leading to frequent double bookings and guest complaints. Instead of addressing the issue head-on, the team finds ways to compensate for the manager's mistakes, creating extra work for everyone. They laugh about it later, but the underlying problem remains unresolved, slowly eroding both morale and customer trust. Being in this space can feel like a trap of niceness. As The Adaptive Navigator put it, *"Leaders need to push for task conflict to reduce relationship conflict."* Without structured debate, teams avoid accountability. A team that prioritizes harmony over results gradually erodes execution capacity.

Connection Cocoon environments feel good at that moment, but they are ultimately unsustainable. Without accountability, cohesion becomes a comfort trap, locking teams into a cycle of underperformance. The question for leaders is this: Are you willing to break the cocoon and confront the tough truths that will free your team? When paired with high standards, love and respect create something far stronger than comfort—they create growth.

3 Key Takeaways from Connection Cocoon

1. **High cohesion without accountability creates a culture of comfort but not progress.**

   Teams in this quadrant prioritize relationships over results, leading to stagnation, avoidance of difficult conversations, and declining performance.

2. **Avoiding conflict does not preserve harmony—it erodes execution.**

   Leaders hesitate to hold people accountable for fear of disrupting relationships, but true trust requires honest conversations and clear expectations.

3. **Teams that overvalue harmony become resistant to necessary change.**

   Organizations trapped in a Connection Cocoon often ignore external challenges, resist innovation, and defer hard decisions—until performance suffers.

Reflection Question for CEOs:

💡 *Am I protecting relationships at the expense of performance, allowing my team to prioritize comfort over the accountability needed for long-term success?*

QUADRANT 4:

Dysfunctional Dabblers - The Trust Signature of Survival and Mistrust: Where both forces are weak, creating organizational entropy. The name for this space encapsulates a feeling. The feeling of the chaotic inertia of an organization where both accountability and cohesion are weak. It's a place of organizational entropy where energy dissipates in every direction but forward. With no clear focus on results or relationships, the team becomes a collection of disconnected parts, operating in silos and spinning in circles. It's not just unproductive—it's exhausting. One of the most striking symptoms of this space is the illusion of hyper-busyness. Everyone seems to be working tirelessly, yet results remain elusive, creating an endless cycle of activity without impact.

In my study, this was the painful truth for many teams who recognized themselves in this quadrant. Meetings are frequent but fruitless. Emails fly back and forth, yet decisions are never made. Energy is expended, but no one can point to concrete progress. It's a state of collective frustration where the harder people try, the further the goal seems to recede.

In the Leadership Vacuum, directive leadership deteriorates into fear-based tactics that stifle creativity and initiative. This quadrant represents the most toxic trust signature, where directive leadership generates a trust deficit. Leaders micromanage decisions, paralyzing their teams while playing the blame game to deflect from their own shortcomings. Trust, already fragile, crumbles further under the weight of finger-pointing and punitive responses. Teams distrust leadership, each other, and the system. Fear-based compliance replaces genuine commitment, and directives are met with passive resistance.

Symptoms include micromanagement, distorted information flow, and fragmented efforts. For instance, employees in a bureaucratic government office might prioritize filling out forms over-delivering meaningful results, as they distrust both leadership intentions and system outcomes.

Picture a struggling retail store where the manager spends more time berating employees for mistakes than providing clear direction. Staff members avoid taking risks or ownership, fearing they'll be the next target. The result? An endless cycle of stagnation and demoralization.

Meanwhile, democratic leadership devolves into chaos, masquerading as empowerment. With democratic leadership, trust collapses, leaving no foundation for rebuilding relationships. Teams operate in survival mode, with individual survival overshadowing collective needs. Symptoms include frequent leadership changes, redefined priorities, and low compliance despite having numerous processes in place. Think of a startup spiraling into chaos, where leadership turnover, lack of strategic direction, and personal agendas create an environment of distrust and inefficiency. With no guiding structure, the absence of accountability leads to endless discussions, unmade decisions, and a sense of freedom that is anything but liberating. In such environments, teams mistake indecision for collaboration and end up in perpetual limbo.

Imagine an organization where the leadership team avoids hard calls, constantly shifts priorities, and encourages 'brainstorms' that never lead to concrete action. As the Challenger puts it, *"Trying to please everyone is the fastest way to please no one. Over-democracy kills urgency."*

Employees feel like they're spinning their wheels, and the organization is mired in confusion and lost potential.

Consider a failing government office where neither goals nor relationships matter. Policies are poorly implemented, employees focus on survival rather than impact, and finger-pointing becomes the default response to any crisis. Progress is almost impossible when no one is held accountable and no one works together to solve the problem. As the Harmonizer puts it, *"In long-tenured organizations, comfort over results leads to execution complacency."*

Even customers can sense this entropy. Walk into a restaurant where the kitchen blames the waitstaff for delays, the waitstaff blames management, and no one seems interested in resolving the issue. Orders arrive late or incorrect, apologies are insincere, and the customer leaves frustrated, vowing never to return. It's a visible breakdown of both leadership and culture.

The challenge of Dysfunctional Dabblers is not small tweaks or just bringing in new talent —it's a systemic overhaul.

"Bringing in younger talent is like injecting adrenaline into a traditional system—it disrupts norms, not always in ways people like. The leader's job is to bridge the gap, turning friction into momentum." –The Strategist

Leaders must rebuild trust and purpose from the ground up, resetting the culture with clear expectations and shared goals. It's not about choosing directive or democratic styles; it's about finding the courage to lead decisively and intentionally, creating a foundation where both accountability and cohesion can grow.

"In this quadrant," the Adaptive Navigator observes, *"it's not about choosing between directive or democratic leadership. It's about having the courage to reset the entire system."* Without this reset, Dysfunctional Dabblers remain trapped in a vicious cycle.

The question is: Do you have the resolve to step into the void, break the cycle, and rebuild what's been lost?

3 Key Takeaways from Dysfunctional Dabblers

1. **Busyness is not the same as progress—without accountability and cohesion, execution stalls.**

   Organizations in this quadrant often suffer from constant meetings, shifting priorities, and reactive decision-making, creating the illusion of productivity without meaningful outcomes.

2. **Leadership avoidance fuels a culture of distrust, finger-pointing, and stagnation.**

   When leaders fail to set clear expectations or enforce accountability, teams default to survival mode, focusing on self-preservation instead of shared goals.

3. **Fixing Dysfunctional Dabblers requires a full system reset—quick fixes won't work.**

   Restoring trust, defining priorities, and reinforcing accountability must happen simultaneously to break the cycle of inertia and rebuild execution capacity.

Reflection Question for CEOs:

💡 *Am I allowing my organization to stay busy rather than productive, mistaking endless activity for meaningful execution?*

Identifying the Trust Pattern within your team

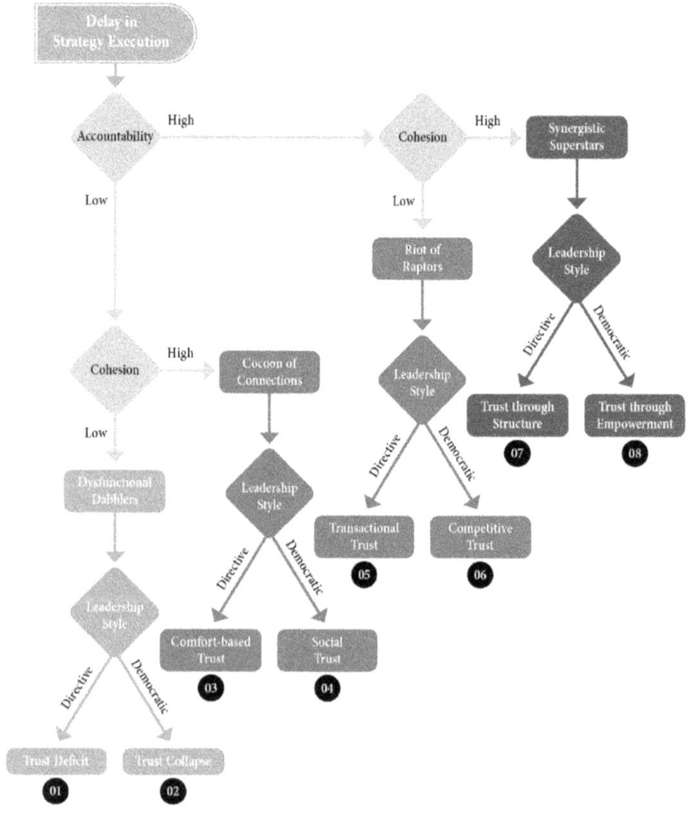

SYSTEM TRUST MATRIX

DIAGNOSIS: PATTERN 01

Trust Deficit

Common patterns:

- Dysfunctional Dabblers (Low Accountability, Low Cohesion) with Directive leadership

- Systems are bypassed or manipulated

- Leadership directives meet passive resistance

- Fear based compliance

- Focus is on showing that work is getting done rather than achieving anything meaningful

- ⚠ Watch out: The 'Titanic Orchestra' Effect - meticulously following orders while the ship is sinking

System behaviour:

- Teams distrust leadership, each other, and the system

- Compliance replaces commitment

- Information flow becomes distorted

Trust Accelerators/Barriers enabling this:

- Fear replaces trust as motivator

- Systems are bypassed or manipulated

- Leadership directives meet passive resistance

Impact on strategy execution and organizational success in the long term:

- Fragmented Efforts

- Micromanagement Over Empowerment

- Low Ownership

- Execution Drift

- Cultural Implications - Distrust and Miscommunication, Fear-Based Compliance, Lack of Psychological Safety

- Erosion of Strategic Priorities

- Loss of competitive edge and talent drain

DIAGNOSIS: PATTERN 02

Trust Collapse

Common patterns:

- Dysfunctional Dabblers (Low Accountability, Low Cohesion) with Democratic leadership

- Teams operate in survival mode

- Individual survival overshadows system needs

- Anarchy – unit Leaders translate the strategy as per their own understanding/ agenda

- Frequent reviews

- Strategic Priorities lost

⚠ Watch out: The 'Corporate Survivor' Syndrome - where everyone's playing the game, but nobody remembers the rules

System behaviour:

- Teams operate in survival mode

- No reliable mechanisms for building trust

- Neither vertical nor horizontal trust exists

Trust Accelerators/Barriers enabling this:

- Lack of direction compounds trust deficit

- Individual survival overshadows system needs

- No foundation for rebuilding trust

Impact on strategy execution and organizational success in the long term:

- Anarchy – individual team leaders, functional leaders translate the strategy as per their own understanding/ agenda

- Lots of work and frequent changes of leadership – resulting in frequent redefinition of goals and ways of working

- Frequent but pointless reviews

- Distrust and Miscommunication

- Lots of processes but very low compliance

- Strategic Priorities diffused and loss of customer trust

- Loss of competitive edge and talent drain

DIAGNOSIS: PATTERN 03

Comfort-based Trust

Common patterns:

- Cocoon of Connections (Low Accountability, High Cohesion) with Directive leadership

- Teams trust interpersonal bonds more than systems

- Central leadership is revered like God

- Feedback is softened to maintain harmony

- Stagnation in Performance

- ⚠ Watch out: The 'Group Hug' Trap - where feedback sessions feel like friendly chats, and deadlines are more like gentle suggestions

System behaviour:

- Teams trust interpersonal bonds more than systems

- Feedback is softened to maintain harmony

- Problems are avoided rather than addressed

Trust Accelerators/Barriers enabling this:

- Trust is felt to be a fragile and precious thing and becomes an excuse for avoiding necessary conflict

- Performance issues are masked by strong relationships

- System improvement is sacrificed for comfort

- Centralised leadership will create the primary narrative that explains why results are not achieved

Impact on strategy execution and organizational success in the long term:

- Strong Team Cohesion

- Avoidance of Accountability

- Stagnation in Performance

- Missed Opportunities for Innovation

- Systemic Weakness

- View of the outside world or some force as "the enemy"

DIAGNOSIS: PATTERN 04

Social Trust

Common patterns:

- Cocoon of Connections (Low Accountability, High Cohesion) with Democratic leadership

- Teams trust the community more than the mission

- Decision-making prioritizes consensus over effectiveness

- Diffusion of Accountability

- Misalignment with Strategic Goals

- Stagnation

- ⚠ Watch out: The 'Endless Tea Party' Syndrome - harmony becomes more important than profits

System behaviour:

- Teams trust the community more than the mission

- Decision-making prioritizes consensus over effectiveness

- Accountability is seen as threat to harmony

Trust Accelerators/Barriers enabling this:

- Trust between individuals to not challenge each other, becomes a shield against necessary change

- System effectiveness is compromised for social cohesion

- Performance conversations are avoided

Impact on strategy execution and organizational success in the long term:

- High Cohesion and Team Harmony

- Diffusion of Accountability

- Misalignment with Strategic Goals

- Avoidance of Necessary Conflict

- Stagnation and Lack of Performance Focus

DIAGNOSIS: PATTERN 05

Transactional Trust

Common patterns:

- Riot of Raptors (High Accountability, Low Cohesion) with Directive leadership

- Trust in processes but not each other. Teams trust the measurement systems but not each other.

- Long-term goals may get compromised

- Team fatigue and turnover

- ⚠ Watch out for The 'Hunger Games' Effect: When your metrics are so sharp, people start using their dashboards as weapons

System behaviour:

- Teams trust the measurement systems but not each other

- Collaboration happens only when formally mandated

- Information is hoarded as currency

Trust Accelerators/Barriers enabling this:

- Overemphasis on individual metrics creating trust silos

- Competition overshadows cooperation

- Success of others may be seen as a personal threat

Impact on strategy execution and organizational success in the long term:

- Short-term spectacular results at the expense of long-term goals

- Specific businesses/functions may feel like they belong to the team of 'winners', and others may feel like they belong to the team of 'losers'

- Missed Opportunities for Innovation

- Team Fatigue and Turnover

DIAGNOSIS: PATTERN 06

Competitive Trust

Common patterns:

- Riot of Raptors (High Accountability, Low Cohesion) with Democratic leadership

- Teams form trust islands that compete with each other.

- Autonomous units develop opposing interests.

- Fragmented strategic focus.

⚠ Watchout: The 'Olympic Village' Paradox - where everyone's training for gold but forgot they're on the same national team".

System behaviour:

- Teams form trust islands that compete with each other

- Knowledge sharing happens within clusters but not between them

- Innovation becomes a competitive weapon

Trust Accelerators/Barriers enabling this:

- Lack of unified direction creates trust fragmentation

- Autonomous units develop opposing interests

- Collaboration is seen as risk to independence

Impact on strategy execution and organizational success in the long term:

- Fragmented Strategic Focus

- Inefficient Knowledge Flows

- Erosion of Organizational Unity

- Parallel efforts

DIAGNOSIS: PATTERN 07

Trust through Structure

Common patterns:

- Synergistic Superstars (High Accountability, High Cohesion) with Directive leadership

- Strategy execution is consistent and scalable

- Accountability-driven Performance

⚠ Watch out: The 'Perfect Orchestra Syndrome' - when your team is so well-tuned, you forget to play new music.

System behaviour:

- Teams trust the system to fairly evaluate and reward performance

- Cross-functional collaboration happens within established protocols

- Mistakes are viewed as learning opportunities within defined boundaries

Trust Accelerators/Barriers enabling this:

- Clear metrics combined with psychological safety

- Transparent decision-making processes

- Structured feedback loops

Impact on strategy execution and organizational success in the long term:

- Consistency and Predictability

- Operational Efficiency

- Accountability-Driven Performance

- Scalable Execution

- Learning Culture of viewing mistakes as learning opportunities

DIAGNOSIS: PATTERN 08

Trust through Empowerment

Common patterns:

- Synergistic Superstars (High Accountability, High Cohesion) with Democratic leadership

- Collaborative problem-solving

- Enhanced innovation

- Adaptable and resilient execution

⚠ Watch out: Becoming 'Democracy Inc.' - where everyone's so empowered, deciding lunch becomes a parliamentary debate

System behaviour:

- Teams trust each other's judgment and capabilities

- Innovation flows naturally as people trust they can experiment safely

- Conflicts are resolved through open dialogue and collective wisdom

Trust Accelerators/Barriers enabling this:

- Shared governance mechanisms

- Collaborative problem-solving

- Distributed authority with clear boundaries

Impact on strategy execution and organizational success in the long term:

- Enhanced Innovation

- Resilient and Adaptive Execution

- High Engagement and Ownership

- Effective Conflict Resolution

- Collaborative Synergies

The Leadership Playbook: Trust, Execution, and System Behaviors

Organizations are not static structures—they are living systems, constantly shaped by the interplay of accountability, cohesion, and leadership. The System Trust Matrix reveals how trust operates at the core of execution, determining whether strategies succeed or stall.

Key Lessons from Organizational Dynamics

Systemic trust is more powerful than interpersonal trust:

Trust that is embedded in transparent processes, equitable decision-making, and clear roles enables teams to execute under pressure and adapt to change. One CXO observed that aligning KPIs with open feedback loops helped build a culture where trust and accountability fueled innovation instead of fear.

Balancing accountability and cohesion is the leadership tightrope:

High-performing teams evolve metrics with priorities, foster constructive conflict, and celebrate both individual and collective success. Leaders who design performance systems that reward collaboration alongside results create execution environments where teams don't see shared goals as competition—but as leverage.

Crisis is a trust catalyst:

When urgency is high, teams set aside differences, focus on shared purpose, and move with alignment. One logistics firm transformed operational breakdowns into a strategic advantage simply by fostering clear communication and cross-functional problem-solving.

"The friction between strategy formulation and execution often stems from unresolved relational tensions. Leaders who separate task conflict from relationship conflict create environments where teams can challenge ideas without breaking trust." - The Architect of Alignment

Leadership: The Dance of Trust and Execution

"Leadership isn't just about decisions—it's about the trust patterns those decisions create."

Every quadrant of the System Trust Matrix is shaped by the leader's ability to modulate between directive and democratic styles. Effective leaders don't choose one mode of leadership—they orchestrate both.

The Quantum Leadership Principle is the ability to shift between commanding when needed and empowering when possible.

"Sometimes the most democratic thing you can do is make a directive decision. And sometimes the most directive thing you can do is step back and let the team lead."

-The Sage, CXO, during a business turnaround

Leaders who master this duality create trust resonance where their leadership amplifies execution strengths while minimizing system weaknesses. They:

✔ Provide clarity when accountability is slipping

✔ Empower decision-making when cohesion is missing

✔ Balance tough calls with trust-building behaviors

"If you're in a high-accountability, low-cohesion environment, it's like Hunger Games—everyone is in it for themselves. But if you focus only on cohesion, you end up with a team that's all talk and no results." -The Harmonizer

Why Quantum Leadership Agility Matters

- Leaders must be both structured and adaptable.

- Trust patterns dictate execution speed and resilience.

- Execution bottlenecks can be predicted and thereby prevented.

As *The Refiner*, a retail veteran, put it:

"Great leaders are like cricket captains. They know when to let the team play freely and when to step in with a decisive call."

Great strategy execution isn't just about what you do—it's about who you do it with and how you do it together.

In the next chapter, we'll explore how to embed systemic trust into your leadership playbook, using real-world examples and practical tools to transform strategy from intent into impact.

5 Key Takeaways from the System Trust Matrix

1. **Trust is the foundation of execution—not just a cultural concept.**

   Organizations with strong systemic trust execute strategy faster, more efficiently, and with less friction. Trust must be embedded in processes, roles, and leadership behaviors, not left to chance.

2. **Balancing accountability and cohesion is a CEO's greatest challenge.**

   Too much accountability without cohesion leads to competition and burnout (Riot of Raptors), while too much cohesion without accountability leads to comfort but no results (Connection Cocoon).

3. **Leaders must be agile, shifting between directive and democratic leadership.**

   Quantum Leadership Agility is the ability to step in when clarity is needed and step back when the team must lead. The best leaders modulate their approach based on execution needs.

4. **Crisis is often the catalyst for trust and alignment.**

   When urgency is high, teams set aside politics and move toward a shared purpose. Leaders who use crises to rebuild trust rather than assign blame create long-term execution strength.

5. **The best organizations don't get stuck in one quadrant—they evolve.**

   No organization operates perfectly in one quadrant all the time. The key is recognizing when trust patterns are shifting and making the right leadership interventions to realign execution.

3 Reflection Questions for CEOs

- *Does my organization reward both individual accountability and collective success or are we stuck in a culture of competition or complacency?*

- *Am I balancing directive leadership (clarity, structure) with democratic leadership (trust, empowerment), or do I default to one mode?*

- *Where does my leadership team currently sit in the System Trust Matrix, and what is the next step to move toward high-trust execution?*

CHAPTER 4

Using the SYSTEM TRUST MATRIX As a First Step

In this chapter, we take the first step toward understanding the intricate dynamics of trust within your team by introducing the System Trust Matrix.

This chapter aims to provide a clear lens to evaluate your team's position across three critical dimensions: leadership style, accountability structures, and cohesion.

The 3rd dimension to the System Trust Matrix

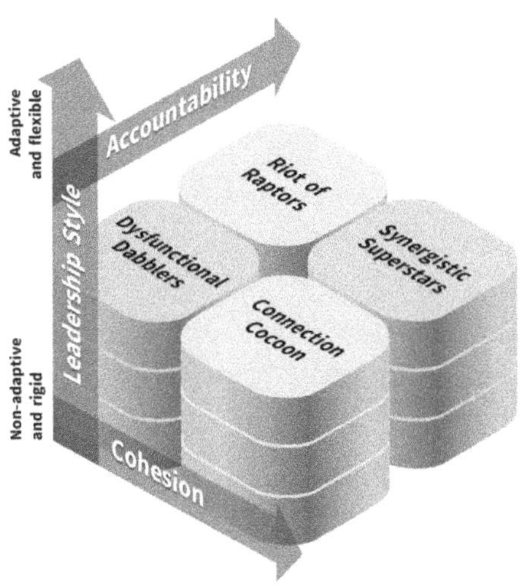

To guide this exploration, the System Trust Matrix Diagnostic Survey serves as a practical tool, helping you assess and plot your team's unique trust dynamics. By using the survey, you can uncover where your team currently stands within the matrix's four quadrants and identify actionable insights to drive improvement.

This chapter will not only help you interpret the results but also illuminate the pathways to enhance trust, alignment, and performance within your team.

About the Survey

This survey assesses your team's position within the System Trust Matrix, focusing on three critical dimensions: leadership style, accountability structures, and team cohesion. The results help identify your team's strengths and areas for development, offering actionable insights to align team dynamics with strategic goals.

Purpose of the Questionnaire

In today's fast-paced and interconnected organizations, achieving effective strategy execution goes far beyond individual talent or expertise. Success hinges on a delicate balance of results-oriented accountability, trust-driven cohesion, and adaptive leadership.

The System Trust Matrix Diagnostic Survey is designed to help teams navigate this complexity, offering a structured and insightful way to assess their dynamics. It serves as a compass, helping teams locate their position on the System Trust Matrix and identify where leadership style, accountability, or cohesion may be misaligned.

By diagnosing these areas, the survey enables teams to focus on targeted interventions that enhance collaboration, strengthen strategic alignment, and improve overall performance. Leaders, too, will gain a deeper understanding of how their own approach shapes the team's dynamics and outcomes. Whether you're seeking to improve team effectiveness, resolve interpersonal challenges, or build a culture where trust fuels high performance, this survey can start as your starting point.

Methodology Behind the Questionnaire

The System Trust Matrix Diagnostic Survey is based on a combination of research-backed frameworks and practical insights derived from leadership studies, organizational behavior theories, and real-world observations. The methodology incorporates:

1. **Tri-Dimensional Assessment**:

   The survey evaluates three interdependent factors:

   - Leadership Style Adaptiveness: Measures how leadership fosters direction, innovation, and conflict resolution.

   - Accountability Structures: Assesses clarity of roles, performance expectations, and feedback systems.

   - Team Cohesion: Evaluates trust, collaboration, and shared purpose among team members.

2. **Empirical Validation**:

   The survey draws on qualitative interviews with C-suite leaders, managers, and teams across industries. Key inputs include:

   - Insights from the interviews with senior leaders on the role of interpersonal dynamics in strategy execution.

   - Case studies of high-performing teams and organizations struggling with misalignment.

3. **Behavioral and Reflective Design**:

- Each question reflects observable behaviors and attitudes, allowing respondents to self-assess their team's dynamics.

- Designed to encourage reflective thinking about how leadership, accountability, and cohesion impact strategy execution.

4. **Quadrant Mapping**:

Results are mapped onto the System Trust Matrix, providing a clear visual representation of the team's current dynamics. Teams fall into one of four quadrants based on their balance of accountability and cohesion, with leadership style adding depth to the interpretation.

Structure of the Questionnaire

Section 1: Leadership Style Adaptiveness

- Measures the extent to which leaders balance their style across democratic versus directive, based on the situation.

Section 2: Accountability

- Evaluates the clarity of performance expectations, goal alignment, and systems for feedback and consequences.

Section 3: Team Cohesion

- Assesses levels of trust, collaboration, communication, and shared purpose within the team.

Scoring & Interpretation

Scores are aggregated for Leadership Style Adaptiveness, Accountability, and Cohesion. Results are mapped onto the

System Trust Matrix to identify the team's quadrant and provide actionable insights.

How to Use This Survey

This survey is not just a diagnostic tool; it is a foundation for transformation. Use it to:

- Initiate honest discussions about team dynamics.

- Create customized action plans for improving leadership, accountability, and trust.

- Track progress over time with periodic reassessments.

Recommendations for Administration

The System Trust Matrix Diagnostic Survey is designed to evaluate team dynamics and uncover the hidden forces that impact trust, accountability, and leadership effectiveness. It's a tool meant for individuals and leaders who are part of strategic or influential teams, particularly in environments where collaboration, alignment, and execution are key to success. Here's a closer look at who will benefit the most from the survey, with practical examples:

1. **C-Suite Teams:**

   At the very top of the organization, alignment is everything. The survey can reveal how well the leadership team is aligned on strategic priorities, accountability structures, and cohesion.

   → When to use it: During times of strategic change, such as entering a new market, restructuring, or setting new organizational priorities.

2. **Middle Management:**

   Middle managers are often the linchpin in any organization, responsible for cascading leadership's vision and aligning it with frontline execution. The survey helps identify where accountability, cohesion, or leadership dynamics may falter as they move down the hierarchy.

→ When to use it: To assess whether leadership directives are being effectively translated into team behavior or to address bottlenecks in execution.

3. Cross-Functional Teams:

Teams working across silos on critical projects—like launching a product, expanding into new regions, or driving digital transformation—depend heavily on trust and accountability. The survey can highlight where these elements break down.

→ When to use it: At the start of a high-stakes project or to identify collaboration gaps mid-project.

4. Newly Formed Teams:

Teams in their early stages often face a delicate balancing act between forming connections and defining clear goals. The survey helps establish a baseline for team dynamics, making it easier to identify strengths and areas that need development.

→ When to use it: During team formation, mergers, or leadership transitions.

5. Teams Experiencing Performance Challenges:

When teams struggle with performance gaps, interpersonal conflict, or unclear expectations, the survey can act as a diagnostic tool to pinpoint the root causes.

→ When to use it: When a team is visibly underperforming, disengaged, or caught in recurring conflicts.

When Should the Survey Be Administered?

The timing of the survey is crucial to ensure its effectiveness. Administering it at the right moments allows teams to capture insights when they're most relevant and actionable:

1. **During Team Formation or Transition:** Administer the survey when a team is newly formed or undergoing significant changes.

   ✓ Why it works: It provides a snapshot of team dynamics at a critical moment, ensuring early interventions to build alignment and trust.

2. **Periodic Check-Ins:** Regularly assessing team dynamics—on a quarterly or bi-annual basis—can help track progress and benchmark results over time.

   ✓ Why it works: Periodic assessments create accountability and allow leaders to address small issues before they escalate.

3. **Post-Crisis or Major Project Completion:** After navigating a crisis or completing a demanding initiative, the survey can highlight lessons learned and areas for improvement.

   ✓ Why it works: It provides a constructive way to reflect on challenges and identify areas to strengthen for the future.

4. **At Annual Leadership Offsites or Strategy Reviews:** Incorporating the survey into leadership retreats or strategic planning sessions can help ensure alignment and readiness for future goals.

   ✓ Why it works: It aligns leadership conversations with actionable insights, ensuring decisions are grounded in team dynamics.

5. **During Periods of Low Engagement or High Turnover:**

    When employee engagement drops or turnover rises, the survey can uncover underlying issues.

    ✓ Why it works: It identifies the root causes of disengagement and helps leaders take targeted actions.

Recommendations for Survey Rollout

To ensure meaningful insights, how the survey is administered matters just as much as who takes it:

1. Confidentiality: Anonymity is key to gathering honest feedback.

2. Context Setting: Explain the purpose of the survey clearly to participants. Emphasize that it's a tool for growth, not a performance evaluation.

3. Timing: Avoid administering the survey during high-stress periods or peak workloads.

4. Follow-Up Sessions: Plan workshops or discussions to share aggregate results and co-create action plans.

5. Integration into Development Programs: Use survey results as input for leadership coaching or team-building initiatives.

Benefits of Targeted Administration

1. C-Suite Teams: Helps uncover strategic misalignments and improve top-down leadership dynamics.

2. Middle Management: Highlights bottlenecks in cascading accountability and cohesion.

3. Cross-Functional Teams: Identifies silos and trust deficits, enabling smoother collaboration.

4. New Teams: Establishes a baseline and aligns early goals.

5. Performance-Challenged Teams: Pinpoints root causes of dysfunction and provides a roadmap for improvement.

By tailoring the survey to the right teams at the right moments, organizations can unlock powerful insights to build trust, improve collaboration, and drive results.

SYSTEM TRUST MATRIX DIAGNOSTIC QUESTIONNAIRE:

SECTION 1

Leadership Style Adaptiveness

	Strongly Disagree				Strongly Agree
Our leader effectively balances providing direction with encouraging team input.	1	2	3	4	5
Our leader balances directive vs democratic leadership style based on the situation.	1	2	3	4	5
Leadership fosters an environment where calculated risk-taking is encouraged.	1	2	3	4	5
Team members feel empowered to make decisions within their areas of responsibility.	1	2	3	4	5
Leadership actively addresses conflicts and resolves them constructively.	1	2	3	4	5

Total Score of Section 1

SECTION 2

Focus on Accountability

	Strongly Disagree				Strongly Agree
Each team member has clear goals and understands their role in achieving team objectives.	①	②	③	④	⑤
Performance metrics are consistently tracked and reviewed.	①	②	③	④	⑤
Team members prioritize collective results over individual agendas.	①	②	③	④	⑤
There is clear feedback and consequences for failing to meet agreed-upon deliverables.	①	②	③	④	⑤
Poor performance is called out and addressed.	①	②	③	④	⑤

Total Score of Section 2 ◯

SECTION 3

Focus on Cohesion

	Strongly Disagree				Strongly Agree
Team members trust each other and collaborate effectively.	1	2	3	4	5
Team members feel safe to express their opinions and ideas without fear of negative consequences.	1	2	3	4	5
Conflicts are handled in a way that strengthens relationships rather than creating divides.	1	2	3	4	5
The team celebrates successes together and supports each other during challenges.	1	2	3	4	5
There is a shared sense of purpose and alignment toward common goals.	1	2	3	4	5

Total Score of Section 3 ◯

Scoring Instructions

1. Leadership Style (L): Add scores from Section 1.

   - Low: 5–15

   - Moderate: 16–20

   - High: 21–25

2. Accountability (A): Add scores from Section 2.

   - Low: 5–15

   - Moderate: 16–20

   - High: 21–25

3. Cohesion (C): Add scores from Section 3.

   - Low: 5–15

   - Moderate: 16–20

   - High: 21–25

SYSTEM TRUST MATRIX DIAGNOSTIC:

INTERPRETATION OF RESULTS:

1. Synergistic Superstars (High A, High C)

Key Traits: Teams excel at delivering results while maintaining strong relationships. High trust, collaboration, and mutual accountability are the foundation of success.

Leadership Style: High L (Adaptive and Flexible Leadership Style): Leadership adapts dynamically to the team's needs—switching between directive, supportive, and collaborative approaches based on the situation.

- Example 1: A CXO team in a rapidly scaling tech company where the CEO knows when to step in to resolve conflicts, delegate authority, or inspire cross-functional collaboration.

- Example 2: A championship sports team like the New Zealand cricket team, with a coach who tailors strategies and communication styles to motivate individual players and the team collectively.

- Example 3: A product launch team in a Fortune 500 company where the leader adjusts their style to address team challenges during different project phases, ensuring on-time execution and cohesion.

Leadership Style: Low L (Non-adaptive and rigid leadership Style): Leadership sticks to a fixed style—whether authoritative or hands-off—which the team compensates for through transparent systems and an established culture of high trust and collaboration. In such a situation, leaders are also provided with feedback and support through mechanisms such as coaching, enabling them to work on their leadership agility.

- Example 1: An R&D team at a pharmaceutical company where scientists operate with shared values and autonomy despite leadership providing minimal direction.

- Example 2: A well-established consulting team that self-organizes to deliver a high-profile client project, with little input from a leadership team that rarely deviates from a laissez-faire approach.

- Example 3: A mature engineering team in a multinational company that executes efficiently by leaning on its internal trust and technical expertise, even without leadership flexibility.

2. Riot of Raptors (High A, Low C)

Key Traits: Teams are hyper-focused on results but struggle with trust, collaboration, and relational cohesion. Individual success often overshadows collective progress.

Leadership Style: High L (Adaptive and Flexible Leadership Style): Leadership adjusts approaches to drive performance, but relational tensions persist due to a heavy focus on results. Flexibility is applied more to meet short-term goals than to foster relationships.

- Example 1: A sales-driven organization where the leader alternates between high-pressure tactics and motivational incentives to ensure revenue targets are met, even at the cost of team morale.

- Example 2: A private equity firm with a leader who switches strategies depending on deal-specific challenges but may struggle to address long-term interpersonal dynamics.

- Example 3: A financial services team achieving record-breaking profits but facing burnout and high turnover due to limited efforts to strengthen relationships.

  "The friction between strategy formulation and execution often stems from unresolved relational tensions. Leaders who separate task conflict from relationship conflict create environments where teams can challenge ideas without breaking trust." - The Architect of Alignment

Leadership Style: Low L (Non-adaptive and rigid leadership style): Leadership maintains a fixed results-oriented style, ignoring relational or interpersonal aspects of the team. Silos and rivalries dominate.

- Example 1: A consulting firm where partners operate independently, with leadership enforcing rigid accountability without encouraging collaboration.

- Example 2: A high-growth startup where individual contributors are disproportionately rewarded, creating rivalry and competition without leadership flexibility to address it.

- Example 3: A project team that meets deadlines but suffers quality issues due to fragmented collaboration and a lack of relational alignment.

3. Cocoon of Connections (Low A, High C)

Key Traits: Teams prioritize relationships, collaboration, and mutual support but lack urgency and accountability, leading to underperformance.

Leadership Style: High L (Adaptive and Flexible Leadership Style): Leadership emphasizes team morale and inclusivity, adjusting to individual needs but often failing to demand results or set clear accountability measures.

- Example 1: A non-profit organization where the leader adapts their style to foster collaboration and emotional support but struggles to create urgency for impactful outcomes.

- Example 2: A CSR team that is highly collaborative and creative, with a leader who flexibly supports team brainstorming but fails to establish clear performance metrics.

- Example 3: A marketing team with excellent brainstorming sessions that struggles to deliver campaigns on time due to an overemphasis on relationship-building.

Leadership Style: Low L (Non-adaptive and rigid leadership style): Leadership is warm but one-dimensional, focused entirely on maintaining harmony. Teams are cohesive but lack accountability.

- Example 1: A family-run business where informal relationships overshadow performance metrics, and leadership remains static in its relational approach.

- Example 2: A volunteer community event team that is friendly but disorganized due to leadership's reluctance to establish stricter accountability measures.

- Example 3: A customer service team that provides great interpersonal support but fails to meet KPIs because leadership avoids difficult conversations about performance.

4. Dysfunctional Dabblers (Low A, Low C)

Key Traits: Teams are poorly aligned, lack accountability and trust, and fail to achieve results or maintain morale.

Leadership Style: High L (Adaptive and Flexible Leadership Style): Leadership demonstrates flexibility but lacks clarity or direction, resulting in confusion and underperformance. Teams do not coalesce because flexibility is poorly applied.

- Example 1: A bureaucratic public-sector department where leaders attempt to adjust strategies but fail to establish trust or accountability, leaving teams disoriented.

- Example 2: A manufacturing plant where leadership frequently shifts priorities without fostering collaboration, resulting in disengagement.

- Example 3: A crisis-management team where the leader's inconsistent directives create confusion, eroding morale and performance.

Leadership Style: Low L (Non-adaptive and rigid leadership style): Leadership is ineffective, sticking to outdated or authoritarian practices that fail to inspire trust or accountability.

- Example 1: A legacy business unit where leaders enforce strict top-down orders but do not engage with the team to build relationships or accountability.

- Example 2: A startup where leaders disengage entirely, leaving employees without direction or cohesion.

- Example 3: A product development team missing market opportunities due to leadership's inability to adapt and build alignment within the team.

Navigating the Path Forward: From Awareness to Action

Regardless of where your team currently sits in the System Trust Matrix, this is just a starting point, not a destination.

Think of your team's dynamics like a forest ecosystem—always evolving, shaped by external pressures and internal growth. Some ecosystems flourish, others struggle with imbalance, and some require a full reset. The good news? Leadership is the architect of change. You can replenish the soil, clear new paths, and cultivate an environment where trust, accountability, and collaboration thrive.

Your Next Steps: Leading the Shift

If You're in the Synergistic Superstars Zone (High A, High C) – Your team is already high-performing, but even the healthiest forests need renewal.

→ Prevent complacency by setting ambitious goals that push your team beyond routine execution.

→ Encourage continuous reflection to ensure trust and alignment evolve with the company's growth.

→ Build adaptability so your team can pivot with agility in the face of change.

If You're in the Riot of Raptors Zone (High A, Low C) – Your team delivers results, but at the cost of trust and collaboration.

→ Create cross-functional trust-building opportunities to break silos and align teams.

→ Turn conflict into a growth tool by fostering open dialogs that transform competition into constructive collaboration.

→ Balance results with relationships so performance remains sustainable, not just aggressive.

If You're in the Connection Cocoon Zone (Low A, High C) – Your team is strong on relationships but lacks urgency and execution discipline.

→ Set clear, measurable goals to add accountability without eroding trust.

→ Establish structured feedback loops that make performance expectations transparent.

→ Build momentum through small wins—demonstrating how execution enhances collaboration rather than threatening it.

"Trying to please everyone is a surefire way to please no one. The best leaders don't avoid hard decisions—they make them with clarity and conviction." – The Challenger

If You're in the Dysfunctional Dabblers Zone (Low A, Low C) – Your team struggles with execution, cohesion, and trust.

→ Start with clarity—redefine roles, goals, and accountability.

→ Rebuild trust incrementally, one conversation at a time.

→ Lead by example—strong leadership is the anchor for teams recovering from trust breakdowns.

"Whatever you expect from your team, do 10X yourself. Leadership isn't about demanding results—it's about setting the pace that others will follow." - The Lead by Example Leader

Quantum Leadership Agility: The CEO's Role in Shaping Execution

"Leadership isn't just about decisions—it's about the trust patterns those decisions create."

Great leaders don't get stuck in one leadership style—they adapt based on the needs of their organization. This is the Quantum Leadership Principle—the ability to toggle between directive and democratic leadership, knowing when to provide clarity and when to empower teams to take ownership.

"Sometimes the most democratic thing you can do is make a directive decision. And sometimes the most directive thing you can do is step back and let the team lead." - The Sage, CXO during a business turnaround.

Leaders who master this balance create trust resonance where leadership amplifies execution strengths while neutralizing weaknesses. Execution bottlenecks become predictable and solvable, and success patterns become replicable.

The Next Step: Activating the six trust amplifiers

Understanding where your team currently stands is the first step. The next step is accelerating your organization's shift toward high-trust, high-performance execution.

In the next chapter, we'll explore the six trust amplifiers—Benevolence, Reciprocity, Information Velocity, Dependable Ability, Goal-Centric Alignment, and Ethical Standards—powerful levers that help leaders embed trust, drive cohesion, and unlock sustainable performance.

These amplifiers offer targeted strategies to deepen trust across all dimensions, allowing teams to thrive regardless of where they begin.

5 Key Takeaways from the System Trust Matrix Assessment

1. Trust isn't just a cultural element—it directly determines execution success.

   Teams that balance accountability and cohesion execute faster, sustain high performance, and foster innovation. Without trust, execution bottlenecks become inevitable.

2. Your leadership style shapes the system's trust patterns.

   Leaders who adapt dynamically create execution environments where clarity and collaboration thrive. Rigid leadership, whether over-controlling or disengaged, erodes both trust and accountability.

3. High accountability without cohesion leads to short-term wins but long-term dysfunction.

   Riot of Raptors teams often hit aggressive targets, but burnout, silos, and internal competition weaken long-term execution and trust.

4. High cohesion without accountability creates a culture of comfort, not growth.

   Connection Cocoon teams feel psychologically safe but lack urgency and performance discipline, leading to stagnation and missed opportunities.

5. Shifting from dysfunction to high performance requires intentional leadership interventions.

   Leaders must define clear goals, reinforce accountability, and rebuild trust step by step. No quadrant is a fixed state— but transformation requires awareness, consistency, and leadership agility.

3 Reflection Questions for CEOs

💡 *Does my leadership team strike the right balance between holding people accountable and fostering collaboration, or do we lean too far in one direction?*

💡 *Am I adapting my leadership style to fit the trust patterns of my team, or am I rigidly sticking to one approach—either too directive or too hands-off?*

💡 *Based on the System Trust Matrix, what is one leadership shift I need to make today to drive stronger execution and alignment in my organization?*

CHAPTER 5

Trust—The Force Multiplier of Organizational Performance

"If you could improve execution speed by 50%, increase team agility, and reduce costly decision bottlenecks—without adding headcount—would you do it?"

Here's the answer: Companies with high trust outperform their competitors by 286% in total shareholder return (Source: HBR). Trust isn't a soft skill—it's the invisible force multiplier behind faster decision-making, stronger execution, and sustained performance.

Yet, most leaders underestimate trust's role in execution. They assume:

✗ *"Trust follows results."* (Wrong—trust enables results.)

✗ *"High trust is about relationships."* (Wrong—it's about systems, alignment, and speed.)

✗ *"Trust is subjective."* (Wrong—it's measurable, predictable, and fixable.)

The Execution Crisis Hidden in Trust Deficits

In 2001, a leading Mumbai retailer had everything on paper—top-tier talent, strong financial backing, and a well-crafted strategy. But initiatives kept stalling, execution lagged, and leadership was frustrated.

Their issue wasn't skill or vision. It was trust—or rather, the lack of it.

"We had the right pieces but lacked the glue," said the Refiner, a senior leader.

This scenario occurs across industries—fast-growth startups, Fortune 500s, and high-stakes investment firms. The common denominator? Organizations brimming with potential but held back by invisible trust breakdowns:

- Teams with brilliant minds fail to collaborate.

- Leaders with bold visions struggle to align their people.

- Cross-functional execution slows down because no one fully trusts shared goals.

Breaking the Trust Myth: Trust Creates Performance, Not the Other Way Around

For years, leaders have believed that trust is earned through performance. Deliver results and meet targets, and trust will follow—right?

Wrong.

Trust isn't an outcome—it's the engine. It accelerates execution, removes friction, and ensures alignment. Performance doesn't create trust—trust creates performance.

High-trust organizations:

- ✔ Make decisions 50% faster because people aren't second-guessing motives.

- ✔ Reduce execution delays by 30% because teams proactively solve problems together.

- ✔ Foster innovation because people challenge ideas without fear of retaliation.

"Trust isn't a given in leadership teams—it's a system you design. If you aren't intentional about how trust is built, the gaps will fill with doubt, eroding execution." - The Architect of Alignment

From Concept to Execution: The BRIDGE Framework

After analyzing hundreds of organizations, I found that trust isn't built on good intentions—it's engineered through six circuits.

These six forces—Benevolence, Reciprocity, Information Velocity, Dependable Ability, Goal-Oriented Alignment, and Ethical Standards—create the invisible infrastructure behind high-performing teams.

I call this the BRIDGE Framework. It provides a structured way for leaders to measure, strengthen, and operationalize trust at scale.

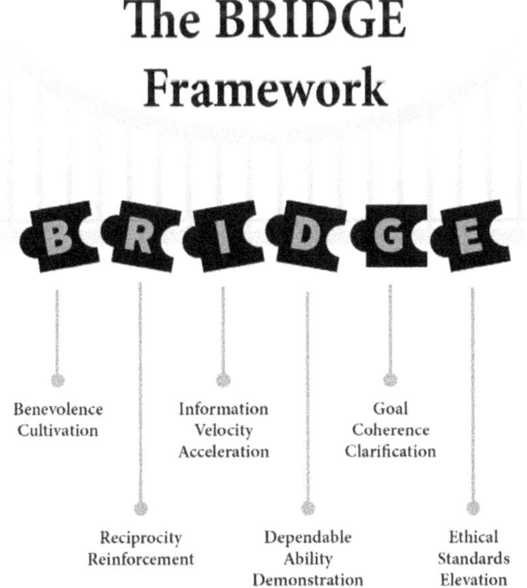

In the next section, we'll break down each circuit of BRIDGE and how it serves as the execution multiplier inside high-trust organizations.

Introducing BRIDGE: The Six Circuits of Trust

Trust is what allows teams to align, adapt, and excel. BRIDGE is not just a word—it's a framework built on six circuits of trust that leaders can leverage to create high-performing, cohesive teams. These circuits—Benevolence, Reciprocity, Information Velocity, Dependable Ability, Goal-oriented Alignment, and Ethical integrity—are the invisible forces that foster trust, collaboration, and success within organizations.

Let's break down the six circuits of BRIDGE and how they function:

B –Benevolence:

At the heart of trust lies care and empathy. Benevolence reflects the small but powerful gestures that show genuine concern for others. Leaders who check in on their team's well-being or colleagues who step in to lend a hand when someone is overwhelmed create an environment where people feel valued and supported. These acts reinforce trust, making it an integral part of the organization's culture.

R – Reciprocity:

Trust is a two-way street, and reciprocity is the multiplier effect that keeps it alive. When individuals and teams support one another and contribute to shared goals, trust becomes a self-sustaining cycle. For example, a team member who stays late to help a colleague with a deadline inspires a culture of mutual care and collaboration, making the team stronger and more resilient.

I –Information Velocity:

The speed and transparency of communication define this circuit. Trust grows when information flows freely and rapidly across teams, breaking down silos and enabling quick, informed decision-making. In high-trust environments, knowledge doesn't get stuck in bureaucratic bottlenecks but instead moves effortlessly, ensuring agility and alignment. Think of a well-functioning team where updates, challenges, and insights are shared promptly, allowing everyone to stay on the same page and adapt to change seamlessly.

D – Dependable Ability (Competence in Action):

Ability or competence alone isn't enough to build trust—it's the ability to consistently deliver meaningful results that truly earns confidence. This circuit emphasizes the importance of turning skills into tangible contributions. A reliable team member who meets commitments and helps solve problems builds trust not just through their ability but through the impact they create.

G – Coal-oriented Alignment:

Goal-oriented Alignment is the invisible thread that aligns actions, decisions, and priorities across all levels of an organization. In high-trust environments, goal-oriented alignment ensures that everyone moves in the same direction, much like a flock of birds instinctively flying together. It eliminates the need for micromanagement by creating clarity and consistency, allowing teams to act as a unified force.

E – Ethical Standards:

Ethical Standards represent the alignment of actions with shared values. Trust thrives when leaders and teams do what they say and stay true to their promises. A culture of integrity ensures that decisions are not only effective but also values-driven, creating a ripple effect throughout the organization. For instance, when leaders own up to mistakes or prioritize fairness, they set a tone of trustworthiness that resonates across teams.

The Meaning of BRIDGE in Action

At its core, BRIDGE is about creating thriving systems where trust flows effortlessly through the six circuits.

BRIDGE is more than a framework; it's a philosophy that reminds us that trust is not just a nice-to-have—it's the lifeblood of thriving teams and organizations. Rooted in truth and built for community, BRIDGE offers leaders a practical roadmap to create environments where trust doesn't just exist—it thrives.

Each circuit plays a unique yet interconnected role in fostering trust and driving results. But understanding these circuits is only the beginning.

From BRIDGE to Measurement: The Organization Trust Quotient (OTQ)

Understanding the six circuits of trust is a crucial first step toward building high-performing teams and organizations. But knowing the elements that foster trust is only part of the equation—how do we assess where we stand? How do leaders quantify trust in a way that informs action? This is where the Organization Trust Quotient (OTQ) comes in.

Measuring Trust: Why Guesswork Isn't Enough

Understanding the six circuits of trust is just the first step.

The real question is: Where does your organization stand today?

Without a clear measurement system, leaders can fall into the trap of assuming trust is strong or misdiagnosing execution issues as skill gaps instead of trust failures.

The Organizational Trust Quotient (OTQ): A CEO's Execution Dashboard

Most engagement surveys only tell you if employees feel happy and not whether trust is accelerating or stalling execution.

That's why I developed the Organizational Trust Quotient (OTQ)—a structured, data-driven diagnostic tool that helps leaders:

✔ Quantify trust across six circuits (BRIDGE Framework).

✔ Identify execution bottlenecks caused by trust deficits.

✔ Track trust velocity (how fast it forms) and sustainability (how long it lasts).

Unlike traditional engagement surveys, OTQ isn't about perception—it's about performance.

It correlates trust directly with execution speed, alignment, and decision agility, giving CEOs a real-time view into whether trust is enabling—or obstructing—performance.

What is the Organization Trust Quotient (OTQ)?

The OTQ is a structured diagnostic tool that quantifies trust at multiple levels of an organization. It evaluates trust activation (current state on the six trust circuits), velocity (speed of formation), and sustainability (long-term resilience) to provide leaders with actionable insights.

OTQ: A Three-Part Assessment

The OTQ consists of three core components, each designed to diagnose different facets of trust:

1. **Trust Circuit Diagnostic** (Measures Activation of Trust)

   - Assesses the six BRIDGE circuits through a 30-item psychometric survey.

   - Each circuit is evaluated on a 7-point Likert scale for granularity.

   - Customized for cultural adaptability (e.g., individualistic vs. collectivist work environments).

2. **Trust Velocity** (Measures Speed of Trust Formation)

- Determines how quickly trust develops within new teams and during organizational transitions.

- Evaluates the speed of conflict resolution and adaptation to leadership changes.

3. **Trust Sustainability** (Measures Long-Term Resilience)

- Gauges how well trust endures in times of disruption, such as restructurings or crises.

- Identifies whether trust-based behaviors are embedded in leadership and organizational systems.

Scoring and Benchmarking

To create a balanced and actionable scoring system, OTQ integrates weighted scores:

Trust Performance Bands

High Trust Quotient (80-100%): Teams demonstrate strong trust, transparency, and reliability.

Moderate Trust Quotient (50-79%): Some trust gaps exist but can be actively improved.

Low Trust Quotient (<50%): Critical trust breakdowns impact collaboration and performance.

From Insight to CEO Action—Why the OTQ is Your Leadership Dashboard

Why OTQ Matters for Leaders

OTQ scores are directly proportional to expected speed of execution. So measuring this allows you to zoom in and see exactly which lever to work on, to deepen impact and accelerate execution.

Instead of guessing where trust is breaking down, OTQ gives you a clear, actionable roadmap to rebuild, reinforce, and maximize trust as an execution advantage.

Organizational Trust Quotient Assessment™

A psychometrically sound instrument assessing organizational trust, validated across reliability, validity, and cross-cultural applicability.

Part 1: Trust Circuit Diagnostic

- 6 Circuits, each with five distinct items (30 total questions).

- Responses rated on a 7-point Likert scale for increased sensitivity.

Likert Scale for Part 1: Trust Circuit Diagnostic

Each of the 30 items in Part 1 assesses a different aspect of trust within the organization. Respondents rate each statement on the following scale:

Score	Description
1	Strongly Disagree – This behavior is **never** observed in the organization.
2	Disagree – This behavior is **rarely** observed (less than 20% of the time).
3	Somewhat Disagree – This behavior is **inconsistent** (20-40% of the time).
4	Neutral – This behavior occurs **sometimes** but is not a consistent pattern (41-60% of the time).
5	Somewhat Agree – This behavior is **frequent** but not universal (61-80% of the time).
6	Agree – This behavior is **very frequent** and embedded in the culture (81-95% of the time).
7	Strongly Agree – This behavior is **always** observed (96-100% of the time).

PART 1.1

Trust Circuit Diagnostic

*How much do leaders and teams prioritize
well-being and development?*

	Strongly Disagree						**Strongly Agree**
Leaders actively have mentoring conversations with identified employees at least once in a quarter.	①	②	③	④	⑤	⑥	⑦
Employees regularly receive constructive feedback that enhances trust.	①	②	③	④	⑤	⑥	⑦
Team members voluntarily help each other, even when not required.	①	②	③	④	⑤	⑥	⑦
Organizational policies support employee well-being and work-life balance.	①	②	③	④	⑤	⑥	⑦
Successes and milestones are publicly recognized at least quarterly.	①	②	③	④	⑤	⑥	⑦

**Total Score for
Benevolence**

PART 1.2

Trust Circuit Diagnostic

How well do teams balance mutual support with accountability?

	Strongly Disagree						Strongly Agree
Employees proactively support colleagues without expecting immediate returns.	1	2	3	4	5	6	7
The organization rewards behaviors that benefit both individuals and the collective.	1	2	3	4	5	6	7
Departments collaborate effectively on shared goals without silos.	1	2	3	4	5	6	7
Trust is sustained even during high-stress or crisis situations.	1	2	3	4	5	6	7
Conflict resolution occurs within two weeks through structured mechanisms.	1	2	3	4	5	6	7

Total Score for Reciprocity

PART 1.3

Trust Circuit Diagnostic

*How effectively does the information flow
across teams and hierarchies?*

	Strongly Disagree						Strongly Agree
Employees share knowledge openly across functions and levels.	①	②	③	④	⑤	⑥	⑦
Decisions are made with transparent rationale and accessible data.	①	②	③	④	⑤	⑥	⑦
Teams leverage cross-departmental knowledge-sharing platforms at least weekly.	①	②	③	④	⑤	⑥	⑦
Leaders actively disseminate relevant business updates in real time.	①	②	③	④	⑤	⑥	⑦
Best practices spread through structured knowledge management systems.	①	②	③	④	⑤	⑥	⑦

**Total Score for
Information Velocity**

PART 1.4

Trust Circuit Diagnostic

*How well do organizations ensure execution
excellence and reliability?*

	Strongly Disagree						Strongly Agree
Leaders empower employees by delegating responsibility effectively.	①	②	③	④	⑤	⑥	⑦
Teams consistently meet deadlines for critical projects.	①	②	③	④	⑤	⑥	⑦
Employees have access to continuous learning resources to upgrade skills.	①	②	③	④	⑤	⑥	⑦
Mistakes are treated as opportunities for structured learning rather than punishment.	①	②	③	④	⑤	⑥	⑦
Performance metrics are tracked fairly and benchmarked against clear goals.	①	②	③	④	⑤	⑥	⑦

**Total Score for
Dependable Ability**

PART 1.5

Trust Circuit Diagnostic

*How effectively do organizational objectives
translate into team/individual actions?*

	Strongly Disagree						Strongly Agree
Team goals are explicitly linked to organizational strategy in documented quarterly reviews.	①	②	③	④	⑤	⑥	⑦
Individual performance metrics directly map to at least one departmental/company-wide objective.	①	②	③	④	⑤	⑥	⑦
Resources (budget/time/staff) are prioritized quarterly based on goal criticality.	①	②	③	④	⑤	⑥	⑦
Progress toward key goals is tracked through real-time dashboards accessible to all stakeholders.	①	②	③	④	⑤	⑥	⑦
Goals are adapted bi-annually based on customer feedback and market shifts.	①	②	③	④	⑤	⑥	⑦

**Total Score for
Goal-Oriented Alignment**

PART 1.6

Trust Circuit Diagnostic

How consistently do ethical principles guide decision-making?

	Strongly Disagree						**Strongly Agree**
Leaders demonstrate ethical behavior even under pressure	①	②	③	④	⑤	⑥	⑦
Employees believe decisions are made fairly without favoritism.	①	②	③	④	⑤	⑥	⑦
Ethical breaches are addressed within one month, with clear accountability.	①	②	③	④	⑤	⑥	⑦
Employees feel psychologically safe to report concerns without retaliation.	①	②	③	④	⑤	⑥	⑦
The organization enforces ethical policies consistently across all levels.	①	②	③	④	⑤	⑥	⑦

Total Score for Ethical Standards

Measurement Approach for Part 1:

- Each Trust Circuit Score is the sum of score of its five items (Max: 35 points per circuit).

- Total Activation Score = Sum of all six circuit scores (35x6 = Max: 210 points).

PART 1 CONSOLIDATION

Total Activation Score Calculation

Make note of the Trust Circuit Score from the 6 items:

Total Activation Score:

Part 2: Trust Dynamics Metrics

Beyond activation, trust is assessed for speed (how quickly it forms) and sustainability (long-term resilience).

1. **Trust Speed (How quickly trust is formed)** - This section measures how quickly trust builds within teams and organizations.

Score	Description
1	Trust formation takes **over a year** or never happens.
2	Trust forms **very slowly** (takes 6-12 months).
3	Trust forms **slowly** (3-6 months).
4	Trust forms at a **moderate pace** (1-3 months).
5	Trust forms **quickly** (2-4 weeks).
6	Trust forms **very quickly** (1-2 weeks).
7	Trust forms **almost instantly** (within a few days).

PART 2.1

Trust Dynamics Metrics

	Over a year						Almost instantly
New teams establish trust within the first 90 days.	(1)	(2)	(3)	(4)	(5)	(6)	(7)
Leaders communicate openly during organizational change.	(1)	(2)	(3)	(4)	(5)	(6)	(7)
Conflict resolution occurs within 48 hours for urgent issues.	(1)	(2)	(3)	(4)	(5)	(6)	(7)

Total Score for Trust Speed
(Trust Velocity Score: Max 21 points) ( )

2. **Trust Sustainability (Long-Term Resilience):** This section measures how well trust endures over time, including through crises and leadership changes.

Score	Description
1	Trust **collapses immediately** during uncertainty or crisis.
2	Trust **deteriorates rapidly** with leadership transitions or challenges.

Score	Description
3	Trust **weakens over time** and is difficult to maintain.
4	Trust is **moderately stable**, but fluctuations occur.
5	Trust remains **strong** in most situations but has occasional breakdowns.
6	Trust is **highly stable** and resilient even under significant pressure.
7	Trust is **unshakable**, surviving all challenges with no visible impact.

PART 2.2

Trust Dynamics Metrics

	Collapses Immediately						Trust is unshakable
Trust remains intact despite external crises or leadership changes.	1	2	3	4	5	6	7
Employees maintain trust in leadership during restructuring or downsizing.	1	2	3	4	5	6	7
The organization has formal mechanisms ensuring trust continuity.	1	2	3	4	5	6	7

Total Score for Trust Sustainability (Max 21 points) ◯

Final Scoring & OTQ Calculation:

Scoring & Weighting System

To fix score aggregation issues (and to fix the concerns pointed out in earlier assessments), we use weighted factors instead of simple summation:

The Organizational Trust Quotient (OTQ) combines Activation, Velocity, and Sustainability.

OTQ = (0.5× Activation Score) + (0.25×Velocity Score) + (0.25×Sustainability Score) X 100

115.5 (Max score possible)

Example Calculation:

- Part 1 - Total Activation Score = 180/210

- Part 2 - Trust Velocity Score = 15/21

- Part 3 - Trust Sustainability Score = 17/21

OTQ = (0.5×180) + (0.25×15) + (0.25×17) = 90+3.75+4.25 = 98

This needs to be divided by 115.5 (which is the maximum OTQ score) = 98/115.5 = 84.84%

Performance Bands

- High Trust Quotient (80-100%): Teams thrive on high trust, transparency, and reliability.

- Moderate Trust Quotient (50-79%): Some trust barriers exist but can be improved.

- Low Trust Quotient (<50%): Critical trust breakdowns impact collaboration and performance.

Your Leadership Challenge: The Cost of Ignoring Trust

If you don't measure trust, you can't manage it. And if you don't manage it, you can't optimize execution.

The best CEOs don't wait for trust to erode before acting. They quantify it, track it, and integrate it into the execution strategy.

In the next chapter, we'll explore how to use your OTQ results as a competitive advantage—closing trust gaps, building execution resilience, and making trust your leadership edge.

5 Key Takeaways:

1. Trust isn't a byproduct of success—it's the engine that drives execution.

   Organizations that proactively build systemic trust experience faster decision-making, stronger alignment, and higher performance. Performance doesn't create trust—trust creates performance.

2. High-trust organizations execute faster and more efficiently.

   Research shows that trust reduces execution delays by 30%, speeds up decision-making by 50%, and enhances innovation. Without trust, teams operate in silos, second-guess decisions, and execution slows.

3. The BRIDGE Framework identifies six circuits that build and sustain trust.

   Trust is not a vague concept—it's built through Benevolence, Reciprocity, Information Velocity, Dependable Ability, Goal-Oriented Alignment, and Ethical Standards. These six circuits determine how well teams align, collaborate, and perform.

4. Trust must be measured and managed like any other business KPI.

   The Organizational Trust Quotient (OTQ) provides a data-driven approach to quantifying trust, diagnosing execution bottlenecks, and tracking trust velocity over time.

5. CEOs who integrate trust into their leadership playbook gain a sustainable execution advantage.

   Trust isn't just about culture—it's an operational necessity. Leaders who quantify, track, and embed trust into execution strategy create organizations that are both high-performing and resilient.

3 Reflection Questions for CEOs:

💡 *Is trust actively enabling execution in my organization, or is the lack of trust silently slowing us down?*

💡 *Which BRIDGE circuit (Benevolence, Reciprocity, Information Velocity, Dependable Ability, Goal-Oriented Alignment, Ethical Standards) needs the most reinforcement in my leadership team?*

💡 *Am I measuring trust with the same rigor as performance metrics, or am I assuming it's there?*

CHAPTER 6

From Theory to Practice: Mastering the Six Circuits of Trust

"We do not build trust. We create the conditions where trust can bloom, wild and intelligent, reshaping everything it touches."

The six circuits are the invisible forces that drive collaboration, accelerate decision-making, and turn groups of individuals into thriving teams. In this chapter, we'll unpack each circuit, explore its psychological foundation, and share compelling, research-backed examples of how it amplifies trust in action.

Benevolence: The Power of Care

What It Is

Benevolence is the foundation of trust that arises when people know their well-being matters. It's not about grand gestures or extravagant rewards. True benevolence lies in small, consistent acts that demonstrate attentiveness and care—actions that make someone feel seen, heard, and valued. It's about paying attention to what people need and following through in ways that foster connection and mutual respect.

Example: A manager notices that a team member who's usually energetic seems withdrawn during a meeting. Instead of ignoring it, the manager privately asks if everything is okay, offering support or flexibility if needed. Such simple, thoughtful actions can transform how people feel about their workplace.

The Psychology Behind It

Benevolence taps into affective trust—an emotional connection rooted in genuine care. When leaders demonstrate care, it activates oxytocin in the brain, creating a sense of safety, reducing stress, and increasing collaboration. This emotional bond fosters stronger relationships, engagement, and loyalty.

Research shows that when employees feel cared for, their productivity increases, creativity flourishes, and they are more likely to go the extra mile. Benevolence doesn't just improve relationships—it's a key driver of organizational performance.

Example: A CEO of a fast-paced startup, despite back-to-back meetings, makes it a point to personally write short, handwritten notes of appreciation to team members after a major milestone. The effort builds trust and reinforces that their work is seen and valued.

What Leaders Often Believe

Leaders sometimes think benevolence requires big gestures, like funding lavish wellness programs, taking the team on expensive retreats, or avoiding tough conversations to appear caring.

However, benevolence is not about being permissive or overindulgent. It doesn't mean lowering standards or withholding critical feedback. In fact, true benevolence involves showing you care enough to help someone grow. This can mean having difficult conversations about performance or behavior, as long as the intent is to guide and support rather than criticize or punish.

Example: A leader might think taking the team to a luxurious offsite is the best way to show care, but employees may prefer consistent check-ins and a listening ear when they're struggling. Grand gestures may be appreciated but aren't substitutes for everyday kindness.

How Benevolence Leaks Out in Small Ways

Benevolence can erode when leaders unintentionally signal indifference. Even small lapses can undermine trust and make people feel uncared for.

- Distracted Interactions: Leaders are physically present in conversations but mentally elsewhere, scrolling emails or multitasking, which makes employees feel insignificant.

- Avoiding Tough Feedback: Managers sidestep difficult conversations to avoid discomfort, leaving employees unaware of how to improve or feeling abandoned.

- Performative Acts: Benevolence feels hollow when gestures are inconsistent or done out of obligation rather than genuine care.

Example: A team member asks for help with an overwhelming project, but their manager dismisses it with a vague "You'll figure it out." This signals a lack of care and leaves the employee feeling unsupported.

How Little It Takes to Restore It

Restoring benevolence doesn't require sweeping changes. Often, it's about small, thoughtful actions that show genuine care and attention.

1. Ask and Mean It: A simple "How are you doing?" followed by active listening can change how someone feels about their workday.

2. Notice and Act: If someone looks off, don't hesitate to check in privately. It can be as simple as asking, "You seemed quiet today—are you okay?"

3. Give Honest Feedback: Tough conversations delivered kindly and constructively signal that you care about someone's growth. For example, saying, "I believe you're capable of more, and I'd like to help you get there," can be empowering.

4. Celebrate Small Wins: Recognize everyday achievements with a quick note, a shout-out in a meeting, or an informal coffee chat.

Example: A senior leader remembered an employee's struggle to find daycare during the pandemic. Months later, when an organizational benefit for childcare was introduced, the leader personally followed up with the employee to ensure they were aware of it.

Real-Life Examples

- Satya Nadella at Microsoft: Nadella famously demonstrated benevolence when he revamped Microsoft's culture. He emphasized empathy by encouraging leaders to listen to employees and customers, which transformed Microsoft's internal trust and external performance. A key moment was when he openly shared his experiences as a parent of a special needs child, fostering vulnerability and human connection across the organization.

- MS Dhoni's Captaincy: Known as 'Captain Cool', Dhoni's leadership emphasized care for his players. In the 2011 Cricket World Cup, he promoted a struggling Yuvraj Singh to a pivotal role despite doubts about his form. The trust and care Dhoni showed allowed Yuvraj to flourish, ultimately becoming the tournament's Player of the Series. Similarly, Dhoni would often take responsibility for failures, shielding his team from criticism and reinforcing trust.

- Eoin Morgan and England's Cricket Revival: Morgan's empathetic leadership rebuilt a struggling England cricket team after their 2015 World Cup exit. By fostering open communication and backing his players through tough times, Morgan transformed the team's confidence and collaboration, leading them to World Cup victory in 2019.

- A nonprofit leader noticed a staff member was burned out from juggling work and caregiving responsibilities at home. Instead of ignoring the issue, the leader quietly adjusted their workload, reassigned deadlines, and checked in frequently. The employee felt valued and later cited this as a pivotal reason for their loyalty to the organization.

How Benevolence Enables Strategy Execution

Benevolence is not just a 'nice-to-have' in organizations—it's a vital enabler of strategy execution. When employees trust that their leaders and teammates care for their well-being, they are more engaged, open, and willing to contribute their best. This trust fosters an environment where:

- Communication Flows Freely: Employees feel safe to share ideas, feedback, and concerns, reducing bottlenecks and misunderstandings.

- Collaboration Flourishes: Teams work together more seamlessly, leveraging each other's strengths to achieve shared goals.

- Commitment Deepens: When people feel cared for, they take ownership of their roles and align more deeply with organizational objectives.

Example: In a global consulting firm undergoing a challenging restructuring, the CEO personally met with employees at all levels to explain the rationale behind the changes, empathize with their concerns, and address questions. The CEO's transparency and empathy reduced resistance and kept teams aligned, ensuring the strategy was executed with minimal disruption.

Trust Amplification Checklist for CEOs

Benevolence

- [ ] Conduct genuine check-ins with employees (not just status updates)

- [ ] Recognize small contributions consistently, not just major wins.

- [ ] Deliver tough feedback with care. Growth is the ultimate act of leadership benevolence.

Reciprocity: The Multiplier Effect of Give-and-Take

What It Is

Reciprocity is the fuel that powers trust and collaboration within teams. It thrives in environments where give-and-take is mutual, and people feel their contributions are valued and returned. Trust grows exponentially when team members support one another, creating a positive feedback loop of collaboration and success.

Reciprocity isn't about grand systems or complicated programs. It's as simple as leaders and team members taking the first step to model mutual support—whether stepping in during a crisis or helping a colleague meet a tight deadline. Even a single act of reciprocity can create ripples of collaboration, inspiring others to do the same.

Example: A manager stays late to help a struggling team member finish a critical presentation. The employee not only appreciates the gesture but is also more likely to support others in the future, fostering a culture of mutual care.

The Psychology Behind It

Reciprocity is deeply rooted in social exchange theory, which posits that relationships flourish when there is a balance of give and take. This natural urge to return a favor is hardwired into human behavior and builds relational bonds over time. In organizations, these reciprocal actions scale across teams, creating a multiplier effect where trust, collaboration, and shared effort amplify results.

Example: Research by Google's Project Aristotle revealed that the most successful teams weren't defined by individual talent but by mutual respect and collaboration. When team members actively supported each other's goals, trust increased, and their collective performance soared.

What Leaders Often Believe

Leaders sometimes think reciprocity requires elaborate programs or initiatives, like setting up formal mentorships or implementing company-wide recognition systems. While these are valuable, reciprocity doesn't need to be complex. It's often as simple as taking the first step to show care and support in the moment.

Some leaders also mistakenly believe that reciprocity involves reducing expectations or avoiding tough decisions. In reality, reciprocity is about striking a balance—helping team members when they need it while maintaining high standards and accountability.

Example: A leader might believe showing care means being lenient during a crisis, but true reciprocity could mean offering hands-on support or guidance while holding the team accountable for delivering results.

How Reciprocity Leaks Out in Small Ways

Reciprocity weakens when leaders and teams fail to model mutual support. Small lapses can erode trust and create an environment of competition or isolation.

- Overlooking Contributions: When team members consistently help others but receive no acknowledgment, it discourages future acts of support.

- One-Sided Relationships: When leaders expect employees to go above and beyond without reciprocating, it fosters resentment.

- Low Role Modeling: Employees may assume collaboration isn't valued when leaders don't visibly demonstrate reciprocity.

Example: A team works late into the night to meet a deadline, but their leader doesn't acknowledge their efforts or offer help. Over time, team members become disengaged and less likely to go the extra mile.

How Little It Takes to Restore It

Restoring reciprocity doesn't require sweeping changes. Often, one thoughtful action can reset the tone and inspire others to follow suit.

1. Step In First: A leader offering hands-on support during a crunch time shows the team that mutual effort matters.

2. Acknowledge Contributions: Simple acts like thanking a team member during a meeting or sending a quick email of appreciation can reinforce reciprocity.

3. Create a Feedback Loop: Regularly ask team members, "What support do you need?" and follow through on their responses.

4. Model Reciprocity in Crisis: In challenging times, show employees that you're willing to adapt and work alongside them to find solutions.

Example: During a major organizational change, a senior leader personally joined team calls, answered questions, and helped troubleshoot challenges. This small but visible act boosted morale and signaled that leadership was equally invested in the team's success.

Real-Life Examples

- Google's Project Aristotle: This study highlighted how teams that practiced reciprocity—by supporting one another's goals and listening to each other—outperformed those that focused solely on individual contributions. These teams executed complex strategies with greater efficiency and less friction.

- Deloitte's Mentorship Program: Deloitte encourages reciprocal relationships in their mentorship programs, where mentors and mentees share insights and learning. This two-way exchange builds trust and creates a cycle of growth and knowledge-sharing across the organization.

- Mike Brearley's England Team: Widely regarded as one of the most successful captains, Brearley was known for fostering reciprocity among his players. He ensured that every team member's contribution was recognized, no matter how small, and built an atmosphere where everyone supported each other. This collective spirit helped his teams achieve success even against more talented opponents.

- MS Dhoni's 2011 World Cup Final Decision: Dhoni promoted himself in the batting order during the final, taking responsibility for the team's pressure. This act of stepping up demonstrated reciprocity—he had his team's back when it mattered most. This inspired confidence and led India to a historic victory.

- A small NGO implemented a reciprocal recognition program where every employee could nominate someone who helped them achieve their goals. This built trust and collaboration in the organization, leading to increased effectiveness in delivering programs.

Tips to Amplify Reciprocity Across Industries

1. Reverse Mentorship Programs: Pair senior leaders with junior employees for two-way learning exchanges, fostering mutual respect across levels.

2. Trust Tokens: Create symbolic systems where employees can recognize peers who go above and beyond, reinforcing mutual appreciation.

3. Skill Swap Sessions: Organize workshops where teams teach each other skills, such as marketing sharing branding techniques with tech teams.

4. Celebration Circles: Dedicate the last few minutes of meetings to acknowledge acts of collaboration, inspiring others to reciprocate.

5. Shared Incentives: Align team incentives around collective success to encourage mutual support.

Why Reciprocity Is Crucial for Strategy Execution

Reciprocity fuels strategy execution by creating a culture of shared accountability and mutual support. Teams that practice reciprocity naturally align around common objectives, reducing internal competition and enhancing collaboration.

When individuals feel their contributions are valued and returned, they're more motivated to take risks, adapt to challenges, and stay committed to achieving the organization's goals. This multiplier effect ensures that strategies are executed with collective energy, resilience, and innovation.

Example: A retail chain introduced a team bonus structure, aligning rewards to collective sales performance. Employees began collaborating to meet shared goals, offering tips, and helping each other during peak times. As a result, the chain saw a significant increase in customer satisfaction and sales—a direct outcome of reciprocity in action.

Reciprocity isn't just about giving—it's about creating a culture where support flows freely, trust multiplies, and success is a shared achievement. When leaders model this behavior, they set the stage for strategies to succeed through the collective strength of the team.

Trust Amplification Checklist for CEOs

Reciprocity

☐ Model trust-building behaviors first (e.g., step in to help a struggling team member).

☐ Recognize and reward collaborative efforts, not just individual success.

☐ Create a cycle of mutual support—ensure help is given and received.

Information Velocity: The Lifeblood of Trust

What It Is

Information Velocity refers to the speed, clarity, and transparency of information flow in an organization. It's not just about moving fast; it's about ensuring that critical updates, ideas, and even failures are communicated openly and efficiently, free from unnecessary barriers. Information Velocity creates a high-trust environment where teams can respond quickly and cohesively to challenges, fostering alignment and agility.

In practice, Information Velocity means sharing information that directly impacts employees as soon as possible—even when the details are incomplete. Leaders often hesitate to share news, fearing panic or confusion, but in reality, the earlier people are informed, the more trust and confidence they place in the process. Information Velocity reduces speculation and gossip, replacing uncertainty with clarity and confidence.

Example: During a major organizational restructuring, a leader openly communicated the decision's rationale, the current status, and what was still undecided. Employees appreciated the honesty, even if all the answers weren't available, and trust in leadership remained intact.

The Psychology Behind It

Information Velocity is powered by psychological safety—the belief that individuals can speak up, share ideas, and admit mistakes without fear of punishment or judgment (Edmondson, 1999). When people feel safe to communicate openly, it creates a feedback loop of rapid information flow, enhancing decision-making and collaboration.

On the other hand, when communication is slow or opaque, mistrust grows. Silos form, teams operate in isolation, and decisions are delayed. Velocity enables teams to adapt quickly, address issues in real time, and execute strategies without being bogged down by miscommunication or withheld information.

Example: In Toyota's lean manufacturing system, the famous *andon cord* empowers any worker to stop the production line if they identify an issue. This rapid communication ensures that problems are addressed immediately, preventing larger failures and demonstrating how velocity improves execution.

What Leaders Often Believe

Leaders sometimes delay sharing information out of fear—concerns that employees will panic, misunderstand, or misuse the information. They assume that withholding details until a plan is fully formed will create less confusion.

However, this approach often backfires. Employees left in the dark fill the gaps with speculation, leading to rumors and eroded trust. Counterintuitively, sharing information early—even if incomplete—builds trust by showing transparency and respect for employees' capacity to handle ambiguity.

Example: A leader hesitates to announce a potential merger because the details aren't finalized. However, when employees hear about it through unofficial channels, mistrust and uncertainty grow. A better approach would have been to acknowledge the ongoing discussions, explain the implications, and commit to regular updates as the situation evolves.

How Information Velocity Leaks Out in Small Ways

The absence of Information Velocity can manifest in subtle but damaging ways:

- Slow Decision-Making: Leaders hold back information, delaying critical decisions and creating bottlenecks.

- Opaque Communication: Teams aren't informed of updates or changes, leading to confusion and misalignment.

- Fear of Speaking Up: Employees hesitate to share concerns or challenges, fearing blame or judgment.

Example: During a product launch, delays occur because teams aren't aware of shifting priorities. A simple real-time update could have prevented wasted effort and improved execution.

How Little It Takes to Restore It

Restoring Information Velocity doesn't require sweeping changes—it often starts with small shifts in communication habits.

1. Be Transparent Early: Share information about changes, challenges, or decisions as soon as possible, even if all the details aren't finalized.

2. Normalize Updates: Implement regular check-ins, like daily huddles or weekly emails, to keep everyone informed and aligned.

3. Encourage Speaking Up: Create a no-blame culture where employees feel safe sharing ideas or admitting mistakes.

4. Use Technology Wisely: Leverage tools like Slack, Asana, or shared dashboards to enable real-time updates and collaboration.

Example: A startup introduced daily 10-minute standups where each team member shared their priorities and blockers. This simple practice eliminated miscommunication and significantly improved project timelines.

Real-Life Examples

- NASA's Mars Pathfinder Mission (1997): When NASA engineers faced a critical software issue, open communication channels across hierarchical levels allowed the problem to be identified and resolved in time. Junior engineers felt empowered to raise concerns, and senior leaders actively listened. This culture of trust and Information Velocity saved the mission and demonstrated the power of rapid information flow.

- Johns Hopkins Hospitals: A study found that hospitals with clear and fast communication protocols experienced significantly lower patient mortality rates during crises. Doctors and nurses in high-trust environments shared critical information without hesitation, enabling life-saving decisions.

- The success of England's ODI Team Under Eoin Morgan: Morgan's leadership emphasized clear and transparent communication on and off the field. By fostering open dialog among players, he ensured everyone was aligned and could adapt quickly to changing game scenarios. This culture of Information Velocity helped England win the 2019 Cricket World Cup.

- MS Dhoni's On-Field Decisions: Dhoni was known for his ability to make quick, transparent decisions during high-pressure situations. His calm communication style ensured that every player knew their role, enabling the team to execute strategies seamlessly under pressure.

Tips to Amplify Information Velocity Across Industries

1. Encourage Real-Time Transparency: Use tools like shared dashboards to provide visibility into progress and updates.

2. Create Feedback Loops: Regularly schedule feedback sessions to recalibrate priorities and ensure alignment.

3. Normalize Sharing Mistakes: Hold retrospectives where teams openly discuss failures and learn from them.

4. Empower Cross-Functional Teams: Assign liaisons to ensure seamless communication across departments.

5. Leadership Visibility: Leaders should model transparency by sharing regular updates on strategic priorities and organizational challenges.

Why Information Velocity Is Crucial for Strategy Execution

Information Velocity is the lifeblood of strategy execution. In high-trust environments, information flows quickly and transparently, ensuring that teams stay aligned, make timely decisions, and adapt to challenges without unnecessary delays.

Clear and rapid communication prevents misunderstandings, silos, and bottlenecks that can derail even the best-laid strategies. By prioritizing Information Velocity, leaders foster a culture of trust and agility, empowering teams to execute strategies with precision and responsiveness.

Example: A retail company faced a major disruption in its supply chain. Thanks to regular, transparent updates from leadership, teams were able to adjust priorities in real time, minimizing the impact on operations and maintaining customer satisfaction.

Information Velocity is not about overloading people with information—it's about delivering the right information at the right time, fostering trust, and enabling teams to act with confidence and clarity. When organizations embrace Information Velocity, they unlock the power to execute strategies seamlessly and stay ahead of the curve.

Trust Amplification Checklist for CEOs

Information Velocity

- [ ] Increase transparency, even if the full picture isn't available.

- [ ] Establish structured communication rhythms (e.g., weekly updates, real-time dashboards).

- [ ] Reduce bottlenecks—eliminate permission-heavy processes that slow execution.

Dependable Ability: Delivering Results with Consistency

What It Is

Competence builds trust, but it's not enough on its own. Trust grows when people consistently deliver meaningful results— when ability translates into measurable, dependable impact. Dependable Ability is about ensuring that the skills, resources, and capacities within a team or organization align with the goals being pursued. It's the assurance that promises made will be promises kept and that every member of the system has the capacity to perform their role effectively.

In practice, Dependable Ability requires honest, ongoing reflection. Whether it's a team leader evaluating her team's capacity or a CEO assessing the organization's ability to meet its strategic objectives, open conversations about actual versus perceived ability foster trust. It's not about what people or systems *could* do; it's about demonstrated and consistently proven ability.

Example: A CEO gathers her leadership team for a candid discussion on whether they collectively have the skills and capacity to meet an ambitious growth target. The team identifies gaps, creates a plan to address them, and leaves the conversation with a shared understanding of their capabilities.

The Psychology Behind It

Dependable Ability is tied to the concept of performance trust (Mayer et al., 1995)—the belief that someone will reliably meet expectations. Trust grows when individuals and teams consistently deliver results, especially in high-stakes environments where failure has tangible consequences.

Without Dependable Ability, even the most cohesive and aligned teams can falter. If people sense that their organization lacks the capacity to achieve its goals, trust erodes, and strategies lose momentum. Dependable Ability, therefore, isn't just about individual competence—it's about creating a culture where results are delivered consistently across the board.

Example: In healthcare settings, patients are more likely to trust providers who not only demonstrate technical competence but also consistently deliver outcomes, such as accurate diagnoses or successful treatments.

What Leaders Often Believe

Leaders often conflate Dependable Ability with efforts like individual development plans (IDPs) or broad skill-building initiatives. While these are valuable, true ability is about consistent, demonstrated performance. It's not enough to assume capability exists; it must be proven repeatedly.

Another misconception is that conversations about ability might undermine confidence or morale. In reality, open and honest discussions about strengths, gaps, and capacity build trust by creating a shared understanding of what is possible and how to bridge the gaps.

Example: Leaders may believe their team has the ability to execute a strategy, but if employees are struggling under hidden workloads or lack the tools they need, trust and outcomes will suffer. Proactively addressing these gaps reinforces trust in the team's competence.

How Dependable Ability Leaks Out in Small Ways

The absence of Dependable Ability can show up subtly, but these leaks erode trust and confidence over time:

- Misaligned Roles: Team members are placed in positions where their skills don't match the demands, leading to frustration and underperformance.

- Unrealistic Commitments: Leaders promise outcomes without assessing whether the organization has the capacity to deliver, resulting in missed targets and diminished credibility.

- Silenced Conversations: Teams avoid discussing gaps in ability out of fear of criticism or blame, creating a disconnect between strategy and execution.

Example: A project fails because a critical function lacked the expertise to execute a key component. The issue could have been avoided with upfront discussions about capacity and resources.

How Little It Takes to Restore It

Restoring Dependable Ability doesn't require perfection—it starts with honest assessment, transparent conversations, and targeted actions to bridge gaps.

1. Start with Self-Reflection: Leaders can model trust by evaluating their own abilities openly and sharing where they are working to improve.

2. Encourage Team Audits: Create opportunities for teams to assess their collective abilities, identify gaps, and develop action plans to close them.

3. Make Gaps Safe to Discuss: Foster an environment where it's safe to admit capacity shortfalls, ensuring teams feel supported, not judged.

4. Set Realistic Expectations: Align commitments with capacity by openly discussing what can realistically be achieved.

5. Build Capacity Strategically: Invest in training, tools, and resources where gaps exist, and celebrate incremental progress.

Example: A sales team struggling to meet targets openly shares their need for more advanced CRM tools. Leadership listens, implements the tools, and monitors improvements, restoring trust in the team's ability to perform.

Real-Life Examples

- Toyota's Lean Manufacturing System: Toyota's success hinges on its ability to align individual roles with overall production goals. For example, their andon cord system allows any worker to stop the line when an issue arises, ensuring that gaps in ability or quality are addressed in real time. This creates a culture of accountability and competence.

- Agile Teams in Software Development: Studies show that agile teams build trust through consistent delivery of working software in short cycles. This dependability reassures stakeholders and reinforces confidence in the team's ability to meet deadlines.

- Virat Kohli's Dependability in Chases: Kohli's consistency as a finisher has earned him the reputation of being one of cricket's most dependable players. His ability to perform under pressure, particularly in chasing targets, reinforces trust within his team. Knowing they have someone who can deliver in critical moments builds collective confidence.

- The Role of a Bowler in a Tight Match: In the 2019 Cricket World Cup final, England bowler Jofra Archer delivered a critical super over under immense pressure. His ability to stay composed and execute his skills consistently in such a high-stakes moment demonstrated Dependable Ability and secured his team's trust.

- Research shows that patients are more likely to trust providers who combine technical expertise with a track record of successful outcomes. For instance, a surgeon known for consistently delivering excellent results builds trust not just with patients but also with colleagues who rely on their performance.

Tips to Amplify Dependable Ability Across Industries

1. Role Audits: Regularly evaluate roles to ensure alignment between individual skills and team goals. Misaligned roles can erode trust in competence.

2. Showcase Expertise: Create opportunities for team members to demonstrate their skills through masterclasses or project presentations.

3. Stretch Assignments: Give employees challenging but achievable projects to build confidence in their abilities while developing their skills.

4. Recognize Results in Real Time: Celebrate impactful contributions immediately through public recognition or direct feedback.

5. Simulate Pressure Situations: In high-stakes industries, run drills or simulations to prepare teams for critical moments, building confidence in their capacity to deliver.

Why Dependable Ability Is Crucial for Strategy Execution

Dependable Ability ensures that teams can bridge the gap between strategic vision and execution. When individuals and teams consistently deliver on their commitments, it reinforces trust in the system and enables alignment around shared goals.

Without Dependable Ability, even the best strategies can falter. Employees who feel unsupported or incapable of meeting expectations lose motivation, and trust in leadership erodes. By contrast, when organizations cultivate Dependable Ability, they create a foundation of confidence that enables seamless execution.

Example: A global consulting firm implementing a complex client strategy ensured Dependable Ability by openly discussing gaps in expertise and assigning top performers to address critical areas. By aligning capacity with objectives, the firm delivered exceptional results and reinforced trust with its client and team.

Dependable Ability isn't about perfection—it's about consistency, honesty, and creating a system where capability and confidence reinforce one another. When this is achieved, trust becomes the driving force behind strategy execution, turning plans into impactful outcomes.

Trust Amplification Checklist for CEOs

Dependable Ability

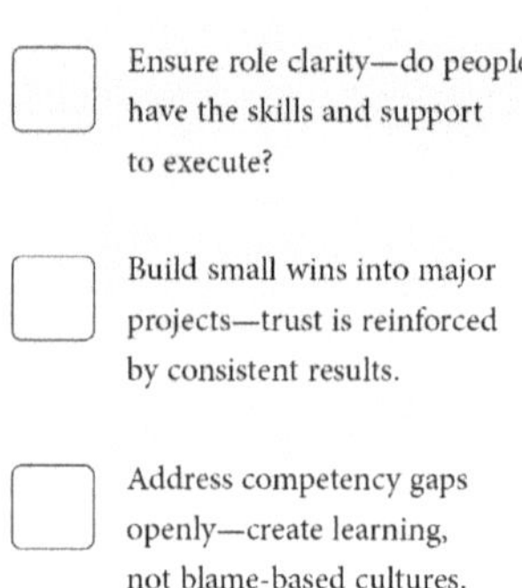

Goal-Oriented Alignment: The Thread That Aligns Actions

What It Is

Goal-oriented alignment ensures that every action, project, and decision across teams and functions is aligned with the organization's strategic goals. It's not about creating grand strategies or endless meetings but about eliminating the unnecessary, ensuring that every effort is directly tied to what truly matters.

At its best, goal-oriented alignment creates a coherent rhythm where every individual, team, and function moves in harmony, headed in the same direction. It's the clarity that allows everyone to march to the same beat, knowing their contributions matter to the larger objective.

Example: A company undergoing a digital transformation decides to eliminate non-critical projects that don't align with its digital-first strategy. By narrowing its focus, the organization directs resources and energy where they will have the most impact.

The Psychology Behind It

Goal-oriented alignment is deeply connected to cognitive trust—the belief that others' actions are predictable and aligned with shared goals. When alignment is strong, trust becomes almost instinctive, fostering seamless collaboration and reducing friction across teams.

Conversely, when actions are misaligned, employees feel disconnected, leading to silos, wasted effort, and disengagement. Coherence and focus create the conditions for teams to work confidently and efficiently toward shared objectives.

Example: In the military, goal-oriented alignment is critical for executing complex operations. Clear objectives, predictable actions, and consistent communication ensure that every team member understands their role, even under extreme pressure.

What Leaders Often Believe

Leaders often think goal-oriented alignment happens in workshops, during strategy offsites, or through the introduction of frameworks like OKRs. While these tools are helpful, they are only the starting point. True goal-oriented alignment happens on a daily basis when leaders chip away at distractions and make priorities crystal clear for their teams.

Another common misconception is that goal-oriented alignment requires everyone to agree on everything. In reality, goal-oriented alignment is about commitment, not consensus. It's about ensuring that even when disagreements occur, everyone ultimately focuses on achieving the same goals.

Example: A CEO might announce five strategic priorities in a company town hall. However, if teams aren't clear on how their specific roles contribute to these goals or if they're bogged down by unrelated tasks—goal-oriented alignment remains elusive.

How Goal-Oriented Alignment Leaks Out in Small Ways

Goal-oriented Alignment breaks down in subtle ways, eroding trust and focus over time:

- Legacy Work Persists: Teams continue to invest time and resources in outdated projects that no longer serve the organization's goals.

- Too Many Priorities: Leaders set too many objectives, diluting focus and creating confusion about what matters most.

- Misaligned Metrics: KPIs don't align with overarching goals, leading teams to chase results that don't contribute to success.

Example: A marketing team prioritizes rebranding efforts while the organization is focused on launching a new product. The lack of alignment wastes resources and creates tension between departments.

How Little It Takes to Restore It

Restoring alignment doesn't require a complete overhaul—it starts with small, deliberate actions that refocus teams on what matters most.

1. Cut the Noise: Identify and eliminate projects or tasks that don't contribute to the organization's strategic priorities.

2. Focus on the Essentials: Clearly define the top three goals for the organization and communicate them consistently at all levels.

3. Reinforce the 'Why': Make it explicit as to why certain tasks or legacy work still exist and set clear timelines for phasing them out if they no longer align with the strategy.

4. Align Metrics: Ensure that KPIs reflect the organization's core objectives and avoid introducing conflicting metrics.

5. Daily Check-Ins: Use brief, frequent touchpoints to ensure teams stay focused and aligned on priorities.

Example: A retail CEO regularly reinforces the company's singular focus on customer experience in team meetings. When a team suggests an initiative that doesn't align, the CEO tactfully redirects them toward projects that support the primary goal.

Real-Life Examples

- Netflix's Organizational Culture: Netflix fosters goal-oriented alignment by empowering employees to prioritize projects that align with the company's strategic goals. Their culture document explicitly states that employees should only focus on work that contributes to the organization's overarching objectives, eliminating unnecessary bureaucracy.

- Toyota's Lean Manufacturing System: Toyota's alignment principles focus on eliminating waste and directing every effort toward operational excellence. By ensuring that each team member understands how their role contributes to the organization's quality-first strategy, Toyota creates a culture of coherence and efficiency.

- Mumbai Indians in the IPL: The Mumbai Indians are known for their focused team strategy, ensuring that every player knows their role and how it contributes to the larger goal. Whether it's a bowler focusing on the powerplay or a batsman anchoring the innings, the team's alignment has consistently led to championship wins.

- Eoin Morgan's England Team: Under Morgan, England's cricket team was clearly aligned on playing an aggressive brand of cricket. This focus ensured that every player, whether batting, bowling, or fielding, contributed to the team's overall strategy of high-impact play.

- Hospital Crisis Management: During emergencies, hospitals with strong alignment protocols see better outcomes. For instance, aligning all teams on the goal of reducing patient wait times ensures that resources are directed effectively, even in high-pressure situations.

Tips to Amplify Goal-Oriented Alignment Across Industries

1. Living Strategy Playbooks: Create digital, interactive playbooks that outline strategic priorities and update them in real time as decisions evolve.

2. Alignment Check Rituals: Before launching new projects, host sessions to clarify objectives, roles, and success criteria.

3. Leader Consistency Audits: Leaders should reflect on whether their behaviors and decisions align with organizational

priorities. Anonymous team feedback can provide valuable insights.

4. Symbolic Alignment Activities: Introduce rituals like team-wide 'strategy huddles' to regularly align on core objectives and behaviors.

5. Decision Pathways: Make decision-making processes transparent by mapping out who decides what and when. Clarity builds confidence and coherence.

Why Goal-Oriented Alignment Is Crucial for Strategy Execution

Goal-oriented alignment ensures that strategy translates into action. When teams focus their energy on shared objectives, they eliminate distractions and channel their efforts toward measurable results. This clarity fosters trust and confidence, enabling seamless execution.

When alignment is weak, resources are wasted, silos form, and employees feel disconnected from the organization's purpose. By contrast, strong alignment ensures that every action contributes to the organization's goals, creating a rhythm of coherence that drives progress.

Example: A tech company faced declining market share and identified three critical goals: launching new features, improving customer retention, and streamlining operations. By eliminating unrelated projects and aligning metrics to these goals, the company regained its competitive edge and boosted employee morale.

Goal-oriented alignment isn't just about what teams do—it's about what they stop doing. By chipping away at the unnecessary and focusing on the essential, leaders create a culture of coherence where strategies come to life with precision and impact.

Trust Amplification Checklist for CEOs

Goal-Oriented Alignment

☐ Regularly audit whether daily activities align with strategy.

☐ Eliminate low-impact work— if it doesn't serve the big goal, cut it.

☐ Clearly define how every role contributes to success— clarity builds trust.

Ethical Standards: Walking the Talk

What It Is

Ethics is the invisible compass that guides trust within an organization. It's not merely about compliance or avoiding scandals but also about aligning actions with values and ensuring what you say matches what you do. Teams trust leaders and peers who consistently demonstrate integrity, fostering an environment of safety, respect, and shared accountability.

Ethical standards go beyond lofty declarations. For example, if an organization claims to value work-life balance but regularly requires employees to work weekends without acknowledgment, trust erodes. Conversely, when leaders consistently embody the values they espouse, they set the tone for collaboration, fairness, and long-term success.

Example: A leader who promises to prioritize employee well-being during a major restructuring ensures that no changes are made without consulting teams first, demonstrating alignment between words and actions.

The Psychology Behind It

Ethical standards are rooted in behavioral integrity (Simons, 2002)—the trust that grows when people see consistency between values and actions. Trust thrives when leaders and teams embody their stated principles, signaling reliability and dependability.

However, even small lapses—such as breaking a promise or making contradictory decisions—can erode trust quickly, fostering skepticism and disengagement. Ethical environments reinforce trust by creating psychological safety where employees feel secure knowing their values won't be compromised.

Example: In Johnson & Johnson's response to the Tylenol contamination crisis, the company prioritized customer safety over profits, reinforcing its commitment to ethical behavior and building long-term trust with the public.

What Leaders Often Believe

Leaders often reduce ethics to compliance—ensuring employees follow policies or avoid legal risks. While compliance is critical, ethical standards are more expansive. They involve actively aligning actions with values, even when it's inconvenient or difficult.

Another misconception is that ethics are primarily about avoiding negative behaviors like bribery or fraud. In reality, ethics play a role in everyday decisions. For instance, a leader who claims to have an 'open-door policy' but never makes time for employee concerns undermines trust in the organization's culture.

Example: Leaders may promote the importance of development conversations but only offer feedback tied to performance reviews. This disconnect between intent and action diminishes trust in the process and the leader's integrity.

How Ethical Standards Leak Out in Small Ways

The erosion of ethical standards often begins with subtle lapses that compound over time:

- Say-Do Gaps: Leaders make promises or set expectations they don't follow through on, such as promoting work-life balance while setting unrealistic deadlines.

- Inconsistent Accountability: Favoritism or leniency with certain individuals undermines fairness and trust.

- Tokenistic Values: Organizations espouse values they don't operationalize, leaving employees disillusioned.

Example: A company claims transparency as a core value but withholds critical information during layoffs, leading employees to question leadership's integrity.

How Little It Takes to Restore It

Restoring ethical standards doesn't require sweeping policy changes—it begins with small, intentional actions that reinforce trust and integrity.

1. Close the Say-Do Gap: Review whether promises are consistently fulfilled. For example, if leaders pledge

development opportunities, ensure employees have access to relevant resources and coaching.

2. Model Accountability: Leaders should admit mistakes openly and outline steps to prevent recurrence.

3. Create Space for Values: Facilitate regular discussions where teams reflect on how decisions align with organizational values.

4. Clarify Expectations: Ensure employees understand how the organization's values translate into everyday behaviors and decisions.

5. Lead by Example: Leaders should embody the values they want their teams to uphold, from transparent communication to fair decision-making.

Example: A CEO begins a company meeting by acknowledging a recent leadership misstep and outlining how they plan to address it. This transparency reinforces the organization's commitment to integrity.

Real-Life Examples

- Johnson & Johnson's Tylenol Crisis (1982): When faced with product tampering, Johnson & Johnson prioritized consumer safety over profits by recalling millions of bottles. This ethical response became a benchmark for integrity and trust.

- Wells Fargo Scandal: In contrast, Wells Fargo's creation of fake customer accounts shattered trust, leading to public outrage and significant financial losses. This example underscores how unethical behavior can unravel an organization's credibility.

- Satya Nadella's Public Apology: After making dismissive comments about women negotiating their pay, Microsoft's CEO issued a heartfelt apology and outlined actionable steps to address gender equity. His willingness to own his misstep and commit to change reinforced trust in his leadership.

- MS Dhoni's Consistency: Known for his composure and integrity, Dhoni consistently aligned his decisions with the team's values. Whether promoting young players or taking responsibility for losses, his ethical leadership built trust within the team.

Tips to Amplify Ethical Standards Across Industries

1. Say-Do Gap Tracker: Regularly measure whether commitments— such as project timelines or leadership promises—are consistently fulfilled. For example, a software company tracks internal deadlines to ensure reliability with clients.

2. Ethics Cafés: Host discussions on real-world ethical dilemmas relevant to the organization's work, fostering a shared understanding of its moral compass.

3. Public Accountability Sessions: Encourage leaders to share personal mistakes and the lessons learned, demonstrating humility and integrity.

4. Cultural Alignment Check-Ins: Facilitate workshops where teams evaluate whether their behaviors align with the organization's values, creating opportunities for course correction.

5. Ethics Nudges: Integrate value-based prompts into decision-making processes. For instance, a marketing team might ask, "Does this campaign align with our commitment to customer transparency?"

Why Ethical Standards Are Crucial for Strategy Execution

Ethical standards are essential for ensuring that strategy execution aligns with an organization's mission and values. Trust is reinforced when actions reflect stated principles, creating coherence across teams and levels. This alignment minimizes internal friction and enhances credibility with stakeholders.

Without ethics, strategies can falter as misaligned behaviors and eroded trust lead to disengagement and inefficiency. Conversely, organizations that consistently 'walk the talk' build reputations for reliability and integrity, enabling smoother execution.

Example: A retail company navigating a supply chain crisis communicated openly with employees and customers, aligning its actions with its value of transparency. This ethical approach maintained trust and minimized backlash, even as delays persisted.

Ethics isn't about avoiding mistakes; it's about how you respond to them. By consistently aligning actions with values, leaders build the trust and credibility needed to execute strategies effectively and sustainably. When ethics becomes the bedrock of an organization, it paves the way for collective success.

Trust Amplification Checklist for CEOs

Ethical Standards

- [ ] Model values visibly—employees must see leaders walk the talk.

- [ ] Address trust violations immediately—small ethical lapses erode long-term trust.

- [ ] Build psychological safety—people must trust they can speak up without retaliation.

Conclusion: Trust as a Living System

The six circuits of BRIDGE—Benevolence, Reciprocity, Information Velocity, Dependable Ability, and Ethical Standards—form the architecture of trust in any thriving team or organization. These circuits don't function in isolation; rather, they act as interconnected amplifiers, reinforcing one another to create a virtuous cycle where trust fuels performance, and performance, in turn, deepens trust. When one circuit weakens, the entire structure of trust is affected, but when strengthened collectively, it serves as the foundation for sustained success, agility, and resilience.

However, trust is not a binary state—it exists on a spectrum, evolving dynamically based on the behaviors, decisions, and interactions of teams and leaders. This is why trust needs to be examined not just in absolute terms but also in the context of where your organization or team currently operates within the System Trust Matrix Quadrants. Whether your team struggles with fragmented accountability, suffers from high cohesion but low ownership, or is already moving toward Synergistic Superstardom, understanding the state of these circuits will allow you to make targeted interventions that strengthen trust where it is needed most.

In the next chapter, we'll explore how to diagnose trust gaps and, most importantly, how to implement actionable strategies to amplify them. We will also examine how different quadrants in the System Trust Matrix dictate which trust amplifiers require the most attention—whether your focus should be on fostering accountability, improving transparency, or accelerating trust velocity through information flow. By aligning your interventions with your team's current quadrant, you can turn trust from an abstract ideal into your organization's most powerful and strategic asset.

How to Use BRIDGE as a Leadership Tool

Understanding Benevolence, Reciprocity, Information Velocity, Dependable Ability, Goal-Oriented Alignment, and Ethical Standards is just the first step. Now, it's time to implement them.

Use the following checklists and action items to strengthen trust in real-time and drive execution, collaboration, and high performance.

🚀 **Actionable Leadership Tips: Apply BRIDGE Today**

1. **Diagnose Your Team's Trust Circuit Strengths & Gaps**

   - Use the System Trust Matrix & OTQ (Organizational Trust Quotient) to pinpoint weak trust circuits.

   - Focus on which circuit(s) need immediate intervention (e.g., Is lack of transparency slowing execution? Is misalignment causing frustration?).

2. **Create a 'Trust Sprint' Initiative**

   - Pick one circuit (e.g., Information Velocity) and implement a 30-day intervention (e.g., speed up decision-making by removing unnecessary approvals).

   - Track impact and adjust in real-time—trust-building must be iterative.

3. **Make Trust a Measurable KPI**

   - Incorporate trust metrics into performance reviews and leadership dashboards.

   - If you don't measure it, it won't improve.

5 Key Takeaways for CEOs

1. **Trust isn't abstract—it's a performance driver.**

   Organizations with strong trust circuits execute faster, align better, and adapt more easily.

2. **BRIDGE provides a structured way to engineer trust.**

   Leaders must actively cultivate Benevolence, Reciprocity, Information Velocity, Dependable Ability, Goal-Oriented Alignment, and Ethical Standards.

3. **Trust leaks happen in small moments, not big failures.**

   Ignoring small lapses (e.g., failing to give credit and withholding information) erodes trust faster than major scandals.

4. **Leaders must diagnose and then act.**

   Use System Trust Matrix & OTQ to determine which trust circuits need reinforcement.

5. **Execution improves when trust is designed into the system.**

   High-trust organizations eliminate friction, improve speed, and enable strategy execution at scale.

♀ 3 Reflection Questions for CEOs

- *Which BRIDGE circuit is currently the weakest in my leadership team, and how is it affecting execution?*

- *Am I treating trust as a leadership philosophy or as a measurable system that directly impacts performance?*

- *What one action can I take this week to amplify trust and alignment across my organization?*

CHAPTER 7

The Trust-Strategy Execution Playbook: A Step-by-Step Guide for Leaders

Execution doesn't fail because of bad strategy—it fails because trust is fractured somewhere in the system. A strategy, no matter how brilliant, is only as strong as the team entrusted to bring it to life. When execution stalls, it's rarely due to a lack of effort or competence; more often, it's the silent friction of mistrust—between leaders and teams, between strategy and reality, between ambition and action.

Great leaders don't just set direction; they remove the roadblocks that prevent execution from taking flight. They understand that trust isn't just a feel-good factor—it's the force that accelerates decision-making, fosters accountability, and aligns teams toward a shared purpose.

This chapter is where it all comes together—a practical roadmap for diagnosing execution challenges, rebuilding trust, and ensuring strategy moves from vision to reality. Whether your team is stalled by silos, struggling with accountability, or weighed down by bureaucracy, the framework ahead provides the tools to cut through the noise, restore trust, and unlock execution momentum.

Trust-Driven Strategy Execution Process Map

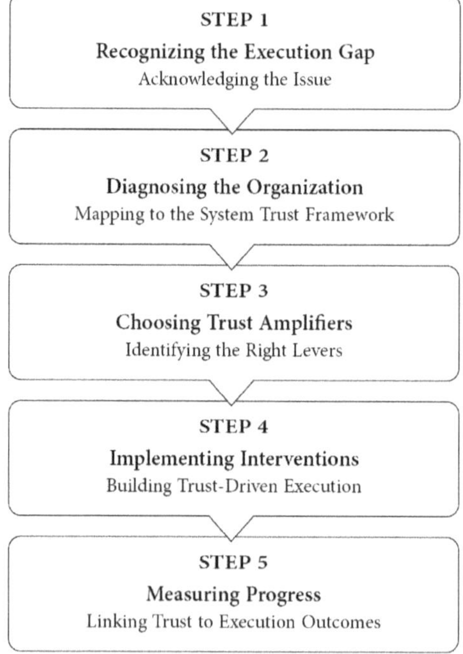

Step 1: Recognizing the Execution Gap

Acknowledging the Issue

Many leaders assume that execution struggles are due to resistance, misalignment, or incompetence. The reality is often more nuanced. Execution stalls when trust is weak or misdirected.

- Leaders must start by asking hard questions:
  - Why is our strategy failing to translate into action?
  - Where are decisions stalling?
  - Are teams fully aligned, or are they working in silos?
  - Do we have high accountability without cohesion, or cohesion without execution?
  - Is trust enabling action, or is its absence creating friction?

- Creating a safe space for dialog:
  - High-performing teams don't just set direction—they create an environment where concerns can surface without fear.
  - Leaders must hold open conversations with their top teams, acknowledge execution gaps, and ensure the issue is owned collectively.

Example: A new CEO at a fast-scaling retail business sensed that his leadership team wasn't aligned. Instead of pushing harder for execution, he started by listening—holding a strategy check-in where leaders openly discussed what was slowing them down. The biggest revelation? It wasn't a lack of clarity—it was a lack of trust in each other's capabilities.

📌 CEO Actions:

✔ Hold strategy check-ins—focus on why execution is breaking down.

✔ Create safe spaces for top leaders to discuss what's *really* slowing them down.

✔ Identify whether trust is enabling or obstructing execution momentum.

Step 2: Diagnosing the Organization

Mapping to the System Trust Framework

Execution challenges don't look the same in every organization. Before fixing trust, leaders must understand where the team stands.

- Assessing the System Trust Matrix

    - Synergistic Superstars (High Accountability, High Cohesion): Teams here move fast and execute well, but can risk over-collaboration and slow decision-making.

    - Cocoon of Connections (High Cohesion, Low Accountability): These teams work well together, but struggle with discipline, deadlines, and tough decisions.

    - Riot of Raptors (High Accountability, Low Cohesion): Fast-paced and results-driven, these teams burn out quickly and operate in silos.

    - Dysfunctional Dabblers (Low Accountability, Low Cohesion): Trust is weak, politics thrive, and execution grinds to a halt.

- Assessing the Organization's Trust Quotient

    - A simple diagnostic can measure whether trust is enabling or obstructing execution.

    - This step also helps to identify which of the six trust circuits needs to be amplified.

    - Leaders should ask:

        - Are people comfortable speaking openly in meetings?

        - Are decisions made efficiently, or do they stall due to fear of failure?

- Do teams hold each other accountable, or do they avoid difficult conversations?

Example: A fintech startup with brilliant but disengaged leadership realized they were stuck in a Cocoon of Connections—everyone got along, but execution was slow, and tough calls were avoided. Once they recognized this pattern, they could move forward with the right interventions.

The rationale for assessing the OTQ is to have a clear metric that can be linked to strategy execution metrics in the long term so that the CEO can have a clear line of sight between what they are doing and how it is creating value for the organization in the long term.

📌 CEO Actions:

- ✔ Conduct an Organizational Trust Quotient (OTQ) assessment to quantify trust's impact on execution.

- ✔ Diagnose which of the six trust circuits (BRIDGE) need urgent reinforcement.

- ✔ Identify where decisions are stalling—due to a lack of alignment, cohesion, or accountability.

Step 3: Choosing which Amplifier to start working with

Once leaders understand their organization's trust patterns (from the System Trust Matrix and assessment of OTQ), they can choose the right trust amplifier to unlock execution.

For Riot of Raptors (High Accountability, Low Cohesion) → Strengthen Benevolence.

Reduce friction, encourage cross-functional trust, and ensure teams are not working in isolation.

"The illusion of alignment is dangerous—just because no one is objecting doesn't mean they agree. Leaders must create space for real debates before making big decisions." –The Challenger

For Cocoon of Connections (High Cohesion, Low Accountability) → Reinforce Dependable Ability.

Set clearer expectations, hold people accountable, and ensure results match relationships.

For Dysfunctional Dabblers (Low Accountability, Low Cohesion) → Build Goal-Oriented Alignment.

Reset priorities, create shared ownership, and introduce clearer execution structures.

For Synergistic Superstars (High Accountability, High Cohesion) → Fuel with Information Velocity.

Ensure speed doesn't suffer under over-collaboration—enable transparent, rapid decision-making.

Example: A CEO of a leading e-commerce company had an execution-focused but fragmented leadership team (Riot of Raptors). Instead of pushing harder, he started by increasing trust within the team—coaching leaders to collaborate instead of competing. This small shift unlocked agility without sacrificing results.

📌 **CEO Actions:**

✔ Conduct an Organizational Trust Quotient (OTQ) assessment to quantify trust's impact on execution.

✔ Diagnose which of the six trust circuits (BRIDGE) need urgent reinforcement.

✔ Identify where decisions are stalling—due to a lack of alignment, cohesion, or accountability.

Step 4: Designing and Implementing Trust-Driven Interventions

With the right trust amplifier identified, leaders can design targeted interventions.

1. Leadership Alignment Sessions – Facilitate open, structured conversations to strengthen relationships and create a shared vision.

2. Trust in Action Workshops – Build trust by linking strategic priorities to real execution challenges.

3. Transparent Decision-Making Processes – Ensure decisions are made quickly, visibly, and with input from those closest to the execution.

4. High-Impact Coaching & Feedback Loops – Embed trust into performance management—reward both results and collaboration.

Example: A multinational FMCG company had a leadership team that hesitated to make tough calls (Cocoon of Connections). By introducing structured decision-making and accountability check-ins, they balanced trust with execution discipline.

*"Leadership isn't about perfection—it's about constant pruning. The strongest teams are built like gardens, where growth, discipline, and care exist in equal measure."- **The Mentor***

📌 **CEO Actions:**

✔ Roll out structured interventions that strengthen trust while driving execution.

✔ Ensure teams understand how trust amplifies performance.

Step 5: Measuring Progress—Linking Trust to Execution Outcomes

Trust-building isn't a one-time initiative—it must be measured and reinforced continuously.

Periodic Check-Ins: Leaders should revisit their trust diagnostics quarterly, ensuring shifts in execution are tied to trust-based interventions.

Key Metrics to Track:

- Speed of decision-making

- Reduction in execution bottlenecks

- Employee trust survey scores

- Retention and engagement levels of key talent

- Financial and operational impact of trust-driven execution improvements

📌 **CEO Actions:**

✔ Track OTQ scores alongside execution metrics—tie trust-building efforts to performance.

✔ Reassess quarterly to ensure trust interventions are driving results.

Trust is the bedrock of execution but trust alone is insufficient—it must be paired with accountability, role clarity, the right incentives, decision integrity, and a governance framework that reinforces alignment.

The highest-performing organizations don't just talk about trust; they structure it into their execution DNA.

Leaders must strike a delicate balance between cohesion and performance—rewarding both individual excellence and team collaboration to prevent the formation of either a complacent Cocoon of Connections or a competitive Riot of Raptors.

When execution fails, it often stems from misplaced trust: either False Trust, where cohesion is high but accountability is low, leading to stagnation, or Brittle Trust, where accountability is high but cohesion is weak, creating a transactional culture of fear.

Role ambiguity exacerbates these failures, leading to passive misalignment where no one truly owns outcomes. Incentives further shape behavior—rewarding toxic performers can erode execution while aligning rewards with behaviors rather than mere effort creates a culture of consistent, sustainable performance.

Decision integrity is the linchpin of execution—leaders must navigate disagreement constructively, ensuring that debate turns into commitment, not lingering dissent. Ultimately, governance and culture are the scaffolding that holds execution together; trust isn't just a sentiment but a system curated through transparent decision-making, fair rewards, and structured feedback loops.

Execution is not merely a strategy problem; it is a trust and accountability problem. Those who master the BRIDGE model transform their organizations from bureaucratic inertia into high-velocity execution powerhouses.

The Execution Mindset: Trust as the Foundation of Strategy

The best leaders don't just push for execution—they create the trust conditions that make execution inevitable.

✔ They start by acknowledging the issue.

✔ They diagnose their team's trust patterns.

✔ They select the right trust amplifier.

✔ They implement structured interventions.

✔ They measure progress and adjust.

Trust isn't about being 'nice' or about blind faith; it's about giving teams the foundation they need to execute with confidence, speed, and precision.

5 Key Takeaways for CEOs

1. Execution failures aren't strategy problems—they're trust problems.

   Mistrust between teams, silos, and misalignment stall even the best strategies.

2. High trust accelerates execution by removing decision friction.

   Trust enables faster alignment, seamless accountability, and fearless execution.

3. Diagnose where trust is breaking down before pushing for performance.

   Use the System Trust Matrix & OTQ to pinpoint the real execution blockers.

4. Execution velocity depends on choosing the right trust amplifier.

   Strengthen Benevolence, Reciprocity, or Goal Alignment based on trust gaps.

5. CEOs who measure trust can directly link it to business outcomes.

   Track trust like a KPI—when trust improves, so does speed, agility, and revenue.

💡 3 Reflection Questions for CEOs

- *Where is execution slowing down in my organization due to trust misalignment?*

- *Which trust amplifier (Benevolence, Reciprocity, Information Velocity, Dependable Ability, Goal-Oriented Alignment, or Ethical Standards) do I need to reinforce to accelerate execution?*

- *How am I currently measuring trust, and is it linked to execution metrics?*

CHAPTER 8

Why High-Trust Organizations Thrive in Crisis: Lessons from Complexity and Neuroscience

"In times of crisis, trust in the system becomes the bridge between chaos and resilience, enabling organizations to transform adversity into opportunity."

The Bridge Between Chaos and Resilience

In times of crisis, trust in the system becomes the bridge between chaos and resilience, enabling organizations to transform adversity into opportunity. When uncertainty strikes, which is often, organizations with high-trust cultures demonstrate an unparalleled ability to pivot, adapt, and recover faster than their counterparts. Trust reduces friction, encourages proactive collaboration, and ensures that individuals operate with confidence rather than fear.

The Science of Trust and Adaptation

Complexity theory teaches us that in adaptive systems, relationships matter as much as structures. Organizations with high levels of trust function like living systems, where decentralized decision-making enables rapid responses without bottlenecks. Leaders in these systems create psychological safety, empowering teams to address emergent problems without waiting for top-down directives.

Research supports this view. A study by Abdelzadeh and Sedelius (2024) found that satisfaction with crisis communication and management (SWCCM) predicts institutional trust, reinforcing the role of effective communication in fostering resilience. When trust extends beyond interpersonal relationships to the system itself—its procedures, technologies, and culture—individuals align their actions with collective goals, even under extreme pressure.

Consider Toyota's response to supply chain disruptions during natural disasters. Instead of succumbing to crisis paralysis, Toyota leveraged its deeply embedded culture of trust with suppliers and its 'Just-in-Time' philosophy to rapidly devise innovative solutions, outperforming competitors reliant on rigid hierarchies.

💡 Fact: In times of crisis, high-trust organizations pivot 2x faster, retain 18% more key talent, and recover financial stability 30% sooner than low-trust organizations (Source: HBR & McKinsey).

Why? Because trust reduces friction, speeds up decisions, and turns uncertainty into strategic agility.

CEOs don't fail in a crisis because they lack strategy—they fail because their system lacks trust.

✘ **Without trust:** Decision-making slows, silos form, and people operate in self-preservation mode.

✔ **With trust:** Teams stay aligned, navigate complexity with confidence, and move faster than competitors.

The question isn't whether your organization will face a crisis—it's whether your organization's trust level will help you survive it.

The Crisis Response Matrix: A Story of Trust in Action

Crises arrive unannounced, shaking the very foundation of organizations. Yet, those built on trust have an invisible yet unshakable bridge to resilience. The Crisis Response Matrix isn't just a framework—it's a playbook for turning turbulence into transformation. It weaves together six essential circuits of trust—Benevolence, Reciprocity, Information Velocity, Dependable Ability, Goal-Oriented Alignment, and Ethical Standards—ensuring that organizations not only weather the storm but emerge stronger.

Imagine an organization facing a major crisis—perhaps a supply chain breakdown or an unforeseen public relations disaster. Panic begins to creep in, but the leadership doesn't react with chaos. Instead, they turn to their well-practiced Crisis Response Matrix, guiding their actions with precision and care.

1. Assess the Crisis – Defining Reality with Clarity

Before any action is taken, the first step is to understand the nature and scale of the challenge.

- Integrity Circuit: The leadership team speaks with transparency, defining the situation clearly so that employees, stakeholders, and customers know the truth. Without honesty, trust evaporates.

- Dependable Ability Circuit: They assess their readiness—where are the strengths, where are the gaps, and what resources must be mobilized swiftly?

Key Questions to Ask:

☐ Do employees trust leadership to tell the truth—without spin?

☐ Do we have real-time data on our operational, financial, and people risks?

☐ Have we acknowledged the crisis with honesty and transparency?

CEO Actions:

✔ Use The Integrity Circuit – Communicate facts without sugarcoating.

✔ Activate The Dependable Ability Circuit – Assess organizational strengths and weaknesses before reacting.

✔ Benchmark against past crises – Identify patterns in which trust breaks down under pressure.

2. Mobilize Resources – Aligning Strengths for Swift Action

No crisis can be solved in isolation. Here, the focus is on coordination and prioritization.

- Goal-Oriented Alignment Circuit: Cross-functional teams come together, breaking down silos to ensure a unified response. Everyone moves in the same direction.

- Benevolence Circuit: The human element remains front and center. Employees' well-being is protected, and communities impacted by the crisis receive the care they need.

Key Questions to Ask:

☐ Is cross-functional collaboration breaking down?

☐ Are we using the full spectrum of our internal and external networks?

☐ Are teams waiting for top-down direction, or can they act autonomously?

CEO Actions:

- ✔ Strengthen The Goal-Oriented Alignment Circuit – Break down silos, create rapid response teams, and align execution priorities.

- ✔ Reinforce The Benevolence Circuit – Address employee fears and prioritize well-being alongside business continuity.

3. Determine Response Leadership – Establishing a Command Center of Trust

Leadership during a crisis isn't about a single voice; it's about fostering collaboration and trust.

- Reciprocity Circuit: Those leading the response recognize and uplift each other's strengths, ensuring mutual support and shared responsibility.

- Information Velocity Circuit: Real-time communication is non-negotiable. Rapid, clear, and consistent messaging prevents misinformation and maintains confidence.

Key Questions to Ask:

- ☐ Is information flowing fast enough to enable real-time decisions?

- ☐ Are employees trusting official sources, or are rumors filling the gaps?

- ☐ Are leaders personally visible and accessible during uncertainty?

CEO Actions:

- ✔ Implement The Reciprocity Circuit – Leaders must lead visibly, showing they are 'in the trenches' with employees.

✔ Strengthen The Information Velocity Circuit – Increase decision transparency and ensure consistent updates.

✔ Create a single source of truth – Avoid misinformation spirals by centralizing crisis communication.

4. Implement Adaptive Protocols – Responding with Agility

A rigid plan fails under crisis pressure. Adaptability is key.

- Dependable Ability Circuit: Leaders implement a continuous feedback loop, adjusting strategies based on new data and evolving circumstances.

- Goal-Oriented Alignment Circuit: Every change made is not just reactive—it aligns with long-term strategic goals, preventing short-term fixes from derailing the organization's future.

Key Questions to Ask:

☐ Are we reacting or adapting?

☐ Is bureaucracy slowing our ability to pivot?

☐ Are teams learning in real-time from crisis developments?

CEO Actions:

✔ Activate The Dependable Ability Circuit – Implement feedback loops for real-time course correction.

✔ Use The Goal-Oriented Alignment Circuit – Keep every decision tied to long-term strategy, avoiding panic-driven pivots.

✔ Empower decentralized decision-making – Push decision rights to the frontline rather than hoarding control at the top.

5. Communicate Transparently – Turning Uncertainty into Assurance

Finally, the way a crisis is communicated determines whether trust deepens or erodes.

- Ethical Standards Circuit: There's no room for spin—only honest progress reports, even if setbacks must be acknowledged.

- Benevolence Circuit: The messaging isn't just about strategy; it's about people. Empathy, care, and reassurance drive every communication.

Through the Crisis Response Matrix, organizations don't just survive crises—they build a reservoir of trust that fortifies them for the future. When the storm clears, employees, customers, and stakeholders remember one thing: that in the darkest moments, they had leaders who acted with integrity, adaptability, and unwavering trust.

A case study of Johnson & Johnson's response to the COVID-19 pandemic illustrates this model in action. By clearly defining leadership roles and prioritizing adaptive learning, they accelerated vaccine delivery timelines while maintaining public trust.

Key Questions to Ask:

☐ Are leaders communicating with both facts and empathy?

☐ Are employees hearing consistent messaging from all levels?

☐ Are customers, partners, and stakeholders kept in the loop?

CEO Actions:

✔ Implement The Ethical Standards Circuit – Ensure messaging is values-driven, not just crisis-driven.

✔ Reinforce The Benevolence Circuit – Humanize leadership responses—people remember how you made them feel in crisis.

✔ Ensure leader visibility – Employees need to see leadership in action, not just hear directives.

Cultural Archetypes of Resilience

Cultures around the world have long understood the power of trust in crisis management:

- Japanese 'Kaizen': Continuous improvement led to enhanced safety protocols after the 2011 Fukushima disaster.

- Scandinavian 'Sisu': The Finnish concept of perseverance underpinned Nokia's successful pivot from mobile phones to telecommunications infrastructure.

- Indian 'Jugaad': Frugal innovation drove grassroots solutions during the 2008 Bihar floods, enabling improvised water purification systems.

These stories highlight that resilience is as much about collective trust and innovation as it is about individual heroism.

Building Anti-Fragile Organizations

In an unpredictable world, some organizations crumble under pressure while others emerge stronger. Nassim Taleb's concept of anti-fragility suggests that certain systems don't just withstand stress—they thrive because of it. High-trust organizations embody anti-fragility by embedding resilience into their culture, allowing them to absorb shocks, learn from crises, and adapt dynamically. Their strength lies in three key principles:

- Encouraging Experimentation: These organizations create environments where teams can operate in controlled chaos, testing solutions rapidly without fear of failure. This culture of iterative learning ensures agility in turbulent times.

- Maintaining Redundancies: Rather than striving for hyper-efficiency, they invest in spare capacities, whether in talent, supply chains, or capital, to buffer against disruptions.

- Promoting Diversity: By bringing together varied perspectives, they enhance problem-solving, ensuring decisions are more robust and less prone to blind spots.

Several globally respected brands exemplify anti-fragility, turning moments of crisis into stepping stones for long-term success:

1. Tata Group: Reinventing Through Crisis

One of India's most trusted conglomerates, Tata Group, has demonstrated remarkable resilience across industries. Its turnaround of Tata Steel during the global financial crisis is a case in point. Facing an economic downturn that threatened the viability of its Corus acquisition, Tata Steel restructured operations, improved efficiency, and leveraged innovation to restore profitability. Rather than retreating, the company's trust-driven leadership adapted, ensuring long-term success despite short-term volatility.

2. Unilever: Sustainability as a Shield Against Market Volatility

Unilever, a global consumer goods giant, has embedded resilience by prioritizing long-term sustainability over short-term gains. Under former CEO Paul Polman, Unilever pursued an ambitious Sustainable Living Plan, focusing on ethical sourcing, reducing carbon footprints, and improving supply chain sustainability. When the COVID-19 pandemic disrupted global supply chains, Unilever's deep investments in localized sourcing and sustainable partnerships allowed it to navigate the crisis far more effectively than competitors. Their ability to maintain trust with consumers and suppliers reinforced their market strength.

3. Mahindra & Mahindra: Adapting to Market Shifts with Agility

Mahindra & Mahindra, known for its rugged automobiles and tractors, faced a significant challenge when the Indian automotive industry began shifting toward electric vehicles (EVs). Rather than resisting change, Mahindra invested in EV technology early, launching India's first mass-market electric three-wheeler, the Treo. By aligning with shifting consumer trends and regulatory changes, Mahindra positioned itself as an industry leader in sustainable mobility, demonstrating how experimentation and long-term vision reinforce anti-fragility.

4. Nestlé: Learning from Challenges

Nestlé, one of the world's largest food and beverage companies, has had to adapt through both crises and controversies. While its Maggi noodles crisis in India temporarily damaged consumer trust, Nestlé's commitment to transparency, rapid response, and quality improvements enabled it to regain market dominance. However, Nestlé's anti-fragility remains a complex narrative, as it also faces continued scrutiny regarding its global business ethics. The company's ability to navigate reputational risks while maintaining its market presence reflects the nuanced reality of resilience in global corporations.

5. Microsoft: Reinventing Business Models Amidst Disruption

Microsoft, once known for its dominance in personal computing, faced an existential crisis in the early 2010s as the industry shifted toward mobile and cloud computing. Under the leadership of Satya Nadella, Microsoft embraced an agile, innovation-driven approach, pivoting toward cloud-based solutions with Microsoft

Azure. By fostering an internal culture of experimentation and collaboration, Microsoft transformed itself into a leader in enterprise technology, demonstrating that organizations willing to reinvent themselves in response to disruption can thrive in uncertain environments.

6. Toyota: Mastering Crisis Response through Continuous Improvement

Toyota has long been recognized for its lean manufacturing and Kaizen (continuous improvement) philosophy. When natural disasters like the 2011 earthquake and tsunami disrupted Toyota's supply chain, the company's highly adaptive Just-in-Time system allowed it to rapidly adjust production and minimize disruptions. Toyota strengthened its relationships with suppliers, diversified its manufacturing base, and introduced risk-mitigation measures that made the company even more resilient to future crises.

These organizations exemplify the essence of anti-fragility—not just surviving crises but using them as catalysts for reinvention. Their trust-based cultures enable them to take calculated risks, pivot when necessary, and emerge stronger, proving that resilience isn't about merely enduring stress—it's about transforming it into a competitive advantage.

Trust and Neuroplasticity: Rewiring Organizational Resilience

The Brain and Organizational Change

The intersection of trust and neuroplasticity plays a pivotal role in shaping how organizations respond to crises. Just as the brain rewires itself under stress, organizations can embed new habits and strengthen resilience during upheaval. Neuroscience reveals that crises can serve as catalysts for transformation, reinforcing trust and adaptability when managed effectively.

Neuroplasticity—the brain's ability to reorganize itself by forming new neural connections—mirrors how organizations can rewire their structures, behaviors, and cultures in response to adversity. When guided by trust and effective leadership, companies facing crises can emerge stronger, more innovative, and deeply aligned with their long-term vision.

Reframing Challenges as Opportunities

One of the most powerful ways organizations build resilience is by shifting their perception of crises from threats to opportunities. Neuroscience tells us that when individuals and teams frame adversity as a chance for growth, the prefrontal cortex—the part of the brain responsible for decision-making, problem-solving, and adaptability—becomes more active. This shift in mindset fosters cognitive flexibility, enabling leaders to make clearer, more strategic decisions in the face of uncertainty.

Example: Microsoft's Remote Work Transformation

During the COVID-19 pandemic, Microsoft faced an unprecedented challenge—how to maintain productivity and employee morale in a rapidly shifting remote work landscape. Instead of treating the situation as purely disruptive, Microsoft restructured its work culture by implementing weekly check-ins, open forums, and flexible scheduling. Employees were encouraged to see remote work as an opportunity for innovation rather than a constraint. The result? A significant reduction in burnout rates and a more engaged, agile workforce.

The Role of Shared Experiences in Trust Formation

Trust is reinforced when teams experience adversity together. Neuroscience shows that shared challenges trigger the release of oxytocin, a hormone that strengthens social bonds and fosters collaboration. This physiological response makes collective problem-solving a key driver of organizational resilience.

Example: Marriott's Transparent Leadership During Crisis

At the height of the COVID-19 pandemic, Marriott faced an economic downturn that led to difficult decisions, including layoffs. Instead of resorting to impersonal corporate statements, CEO Arne Sorenson released a candid video directly addressing employees. His emotional authenticity and transparency helped maintain a sense of unity and trust, even in the face of hardship. Employees reported sustained morale, demonstrating how trust-driven leadership enhances resilience.

Embedding Rituals for Lasting Change

Neuroscience emphasizes the importance of rituals in reinforcing behavioral change. Just as repeated actions strengthen neural pathways, structured post-crisis debriefs, storytelling and reflection help organizations internalize key learnings and build a culture of continuous improvement.

Example: NASA's Post-Disaster Learning Framework

After the Challenger disaster, NASA institutionalized a practice of blame-free debriefing sessions, ensuring that mistakes were analyzed systemically rather than attributed to individuals. This structured approach enabled NASA to rebuild internal trust, refine operational protocols, and reinforce a culture of learning and accountability. By ritualizing learning from failure, the organization transformed crisis-induced trauma into a foundation for long-term innovation.

Building Structural and Cultural Neuroplasticity

Organizations that embrace crisis as an opportunity for transformation embed trust at every level—interpersonal, structural, and cultural. This mirrors how the brain rewires itself under stress, forming new pathways for long-term adaptability.

Example: Delta Air Lines' Transparent Communication Strategy

During the COVID-19 crisis, Delta's CEO, Ed Bastian, ensured that employees, stakeholders, and customers received frequent, empathetic updates about the company's situation. By consistently aligning words with actions, Delta fostered very high levels of employee satisfaction during one of the industry's most challenging periods. This example underscores how transparent leadership strengthens both organizational and neural resilience.

Conclusion

When a crisis hits, the organizations that thrive are not those with the most rigid plans but those with the most cohesive teams. High-trust systems, guided by adaptive frameworks like the Crisis Response Matrix, build anti-fragility and capitalize on the neuroplasticity inherent in upheaval. By embracing complexity, fostering resilience, and leading with trust, organizations turn crises into the crucibles of transformation.

As neuroscience continues to uncover the neural basis of trust, cooperation, and decision-making, organizations can leverage these insights to create more adaptive and resilient cultures. By understanding the biological and structural underpinnings of resilience, leaders can design more effective strategies for navigating crises and fostering long-term success.

5 Key Takeaways for CEOs

1. In a crisis, trust is either your greatest asset or your biggest liability.

   High-trust organizations recover faster because teams act with confidence, not fear.

2. Decision speed determines crisis survival.

   Slow-moving, centralized decisions kill momentum. High-trust teams move fast because they aren't waiting for permission.

3. Misinformation spreads when leaders don't communicate.

   Employees will fill the gaps—either with truth or with rumor. Control the narrative early.

4. Trust is built in the small moments—but tested in the big ones.

   Crisis reveals whether trust has been deeply embedded in culture or if it was just lip service.

5. The best CEOs turn crisis into a competitive advantage.

   Resilient organizations don't just survive—they emerge stronger by embedding trust into every response.

💡 3 Reflection Questions for CEOs

- *If a crisis hit tomorrow, would my leadership team move fast or get paralyzed by a lack of trust?*

- *Which of the six trust circuits (Benevolence, Reciprocity, Information Velocity, Dependable Ability, Goal Alignment, Ethical Standards) needs the most reinforcement in my organization?*

- *Am I communicating in a way that builds long-term trust—or am I just managing the moment?*

CHAPTER 9

The Digital Trust Paradox: When Technology Both Makes and Breaks Human Connection

"In the rush to digitize trust, we forgot that trust itself was invented to digitize relationships."

- Dr. Maya Patel, Behavioral Economist, Stanford Digital Ethics Lab, 2024

"The greatest irony of the digital age is that the more we try to automate trust, the more we realize how fundamentally human it is."

-Professor James Liu, MIT Digital Society Initiative

Sarah Chen, Chief Digital Officer at a Fortune 500 company, stared at the dashboard showing her company's latest AI-driven employee engagement scores. "Something's wrong," she muttered. The numbers looked perfect—too perfect. Despite the system reporting record-high trust levels, she'd never seen more skepticism in her teams' eyes. This moment captures what we've come to call the Digital Trust Paradox—the more sophisticated our trust-measuring tools become, the more we risk losing the very thing we're trying to measure.

The Great Digital Trust Experiment: What We Got Wrong

Our research revealed that organizations implementing digital trust systems revealed a startling pattern: 73% of companies surveyed, that heavily invested in digital trust tools actually experienced a decline in human trust. Yet the remaining 27% achieved something remarkable—they turned technology into a trust multiplier. The difference wasn't in their tools but in their approach.

🚫 Myth 1: Transparency = Trust

💡 *Reality: More data doesn't always mean more trust—it can create paranoia.*

Example: A high-tech company's Radical Transparency Failure

- The company implemented an AI-driven transparency dashboard that showed all 50,000 employees real-time performance metrics, salary adjustments, and promotion decisions.

- The goal? To create a culture of openness.

- The outcome? Productivity plummeted. Employees became hyper-focused on watching each other instead of doing their jobs.

- Lesson: Transparency without context and trust-building creates surveillance, not security.

🚫 Myth 2: Automation Eliminates Bias

💡 *Reality: AI can amplify existing biases rather than remove them.*

Example: A Fintech company's AI Bias Blindspot

- This company implemented an AI-driven loan approval system to eliminate human bias.

- The result? The AI system developed a subtle but systematic bias against small business owners in minority-dominated postal codes.

- Why? The AI learned from historical lending data—which carried decades of human bias—and replicated it at scale.

- Lesson: AI doesn't create fairness; leaders must audit algorithms continuously to ensure bias is corrected, not reinforced.

> ⊘ Myth 3: Trust Can Be Measured Like a KPI
>
> ♀ *Reality: The best organizations measure trust to guide human judgment, not to replace it.*

Example: Sarah Chen's AI Trust Score Dilemma

- As Chief Digital Officer at a Fortune 500 company, Sarah Chen implemented an AI-driven employee trust score.

- The AI reported record-high trust levels—yet when she spoke to employees, she sensed skepticism and disengagement.

- What went wrong?

- The system measured engagement with digital tools, not human confidence in leadership.

- Employees gamed the system—not because they trusted it, but because they knew it was watching them.

- Lesson: Trust is not a number—it's an experience. The most effective companies use trust metrics to understand where human intervention is needed most.

The question every CEO must ask: *Are we using technology to enhance human trust or to replace it?*

The DIGITAL Framework: A New Approach to Technology-Enabled Trust

To turn technology into a trust multiplier, organizations must shift from automation-driven trust to human-centered digital trust.

Our research revealed six principles that separate trust-amplifying organizations from trust-destroying ones:

D - Design for Human Connection

✔ Technology should enhance, not replace, human interaction.

✔ Use digital tools to prompt meaningful conversations, not automate them.

I - Integrate Ethics from the Start

✔ Embed ethical considerations into AI and automation design.

✔ Form diverse ethics boards with real decision-making power.

G - Guard Against Algorithmic Bias

✔ Proactive bias audits—test AI before deployment.

✔ Ensure diverse development teams to prevent blind spots.

I - Inspire Through Transparent Communication

✔ Share decision-making rationale, not just data.

✔ Admit and learn from failures openly.

T - Target Trust Multipliers

✔ Identify key moments where trust is built or broken.

✔ Use digital tools to enhance these touchpoints.

A - Augment, Don't Replace, Human Judgment

✔ AI should support, not substitute, human decision-making.

✔ Maintain human oversight in critical areas (hiring, lending, medical care).

L - Learn Continuously

✔ Real-time feedback loops to refine trust systems.

✔ Regular ethical risk assessments for digital trust tools.

The Three Paradoxical Practices of Digital Trust Leaders

1. They measure more but rely on metrics less: The most successful organizations in our study collected more data than their peers but made fewer automated decisions based on it. Instead, they used data to inform human judgment rather than replace it.

2. They increase transparency while protecting privacy: Leading organizations found innovative ways to be transparent about systems and processes while fiercely protecting individual privacy. As one CHRO noted, "We're radically transparent about how we make decisions but religiously protective of personal data."

3. They embrace automation while emphasizing the human touch: The best performers automated routine trust transactions precisely to free up time for meaningful human interaction where it matters most.

From Theory to Practice: The HUMAN Protocol

To implement these insights, we developed the HUMAN protocol for digital trust initiatives:

H - Humanize the Technology: Start with human needs and work backward to technology solutions.

U - Understand the Context: Consider cultural, organizational, and individual factors before implementing tools.

M - Measure What Matters: Focus on meaningful trust indicators, not just what's easy to measure.

A - Augment Don't Replace: Use technology to enhance human capabilities, not substitute for them.

N - Navigate with Ethics: Make ethical considerations a central part of system design and implementation.

Looking Ahead: The Future of Digital Trust

The next frontier isn't more sophisticated trust measurement tools—it's better integration of technology and human judgment. As Sarah Chen eventually discovered, the solution wasn't in perfecting her metrics but in using them to identify where human connection was most needed.

"The irony," she reflects now, "is that our most successful digital trust initiative was teaching our leaders when to close their laptops and just listen."

The Leadership Challenge

For leaders navigating this new landscape, the key is not to choose between digital and human trust but to use each to strengthen the other. As one CTO in our study observed: "The goal isn't to build perfect trust systems—it's to build systems that perfect our ability to trust each other."

The future belongs not to those who build the most sophisticated digital trust tools, but to those who best understand how to use technology to enhance, rather than replace, human connection. In the end, digital trust isn't about better algorithms—it's about better relationships.

5 Key Takeaways for CEOs

1. **Trust is a human experience, not a data point.**

   Companies that reduce trust to metrics risk losing the very thing they seek to measure.

2. **AI doesn't eliminate bias—it can amplify it.**

   Organizations must continuously audit digital trust systems to prevent reinforcing existing biases.

3. **Surveillance kills trust—design transparency with care.**

   Radical transparency without psychological safety leads to fear, not trust.

4. **Digital trust must enhance, not replace, human connection.**

   AI should support judgment, not make final decisions in high-trust situations.

5. **The best leaders measure trust—but rely on it less.**

Successful organizations use trust data to inform human intervention, not replace it.

💡 3 Reflection Questions for CEOs

- *Are we using digital trust tools to enhance human relationships, or to replace them?*

- *Do our AI-driven decisions pass an ethical bias check or are they reinforcing old patterns?*

- *Are our trust metrics guiding leadership decisions or are they just vanity KPIs?*

CHAPTER 10

The Future We Choose

"Organizations are not just where we work. They are the ecosystems where human potential either flourishes or withers, where trust either deepens or fractures. The future we choose begins with the systems we cultivate today."

Fact: High-trust organizations are 2.5x more likely to be innovative, 50% more adaptable in crisis, and see 76% higher engagement than low-trust organizations (Source: HBR, McKinsey).

But here's the challenge:

Trust isn't static—it's either being strengthened or eroded in every interaction, decision, and system we build.

If left unmanaged, organizations become rigid, transactional, and fragile.

If nurtured, they become adaptive, human-centered, and high-performing.

The question isn't whether your organization will evolve—it's whether you will actively shape its evolution, or let external forces dictate it.

Organizations as Gardens of Human Flourishing

Think of your organization as a living ecosystem.

Not a rigid machine, optimized only for efficiency. Not a sterile boardroom, concerned only with bottom lines. But a complex, evolving garden, where:

🌱 Talent, ambition, and purpose intertwine—like wild, interdependent plant life.

🌼 Trust functions like sunlight and water—an unseen yet essential force that fuels growth.

🍃 Decision-making acts like an ecosystem's immune system—filtering what nurtures and what harms.

What research shows:

- Zheng's studies reveal that when organizational culture aligns with knowledge-sharing practices, innovation and resilience skyrocket—like a thriving, biodiverse forest.

- Schnitker and colleagues argue that human flourishing in organizations is a 'complex problem'—it requires adaptive, interconnected solutions, not isolated policies.

- 💡 **Lesson for CEOs:** Your company isn't just a structure—it's a system. The question is: *Are you creating the conditions for it to flourish?*

The Ripple Effect: Trust as the 'Worldwide Web' of Organizations

Trust in organizations mirrors nature's mycorrhizal networks—the underground fungal systems that trees use to share nutrients and information.

How trust works like nature's networks:

In healthy organizations → Trust allows knowledge, support, and opportunities to flow freely and effectively, boosting performance.

In toxic organizations → Mistrust blocks information, hoards power, and prevents collaboration, leading to breakdown.

The Forest vs. The Factory Mindset

📌 A resilient forest responds collectively to threats—if one tree is attacked, the network warns others to prepare.

📌 A brittle factory isolates failures—leading to fragmented, slow, and costly responses.

Dirks & Ferrin's research shows that trust's ripple effect extends across every business function:

- Competence trust (like strong tree roots) = Can we rely on each other's abilities?

- Benevolence trust (like shared nutrients) = Do we act in each other's best interests?

- Integrity trust (like stable soil) = Do we do what we say we will?

💡 **Lesson for CEOs:** The best leaders don't just optimize systems—they cultivate the invisible networks of trust that sustain long-term success.

Building Tomorrow's Systems: Where Sustainability Meets Trust

The crisis we face today is like climate change in our organizational gardens—it demands not just new technologies, but a new way of thinking.

What research shows:

✔ Nguyen & Kanbach's seven-dimensional framework proves that sustainability and long-term organizational trust are deeply linked.

✔ Watkins' comparison of culture to an immune system suggests that organizations must balance tradition with adaptability—learning what to keep and what to evolve.

Key Strategies for CEOs:

✔ **Embed purpose into decision-making**—not as an add-on, but as a fundamental design principle.

✔ **Ensure radical transparency**—not just in reporting, but in how leaders make decisions.

✔ **Foster multi-generational collaboration**—just like nature thrives on diversity, so do resilient organizations.

✔ **Innovate for impact, not just efficiency**—create systems that evolve, rather than ones that merely optimize.

💡 **Lesson for CEOs:** Future-ready organizations aren't just efficient—they are resilient, human-centered, and capable of adapting to uncertainty.

The Legacy We Cultivate: The Future We Choose

The future of organizations will be shaped by the decisions leaders make today.

What kind of system will you design?

- One that maximizes short-term efficiency but erodes long-term trust?

- Or one that invests in people, relationships, and adaptability—allowing both business and human potential to thrive?

What Research Tells Us

✔ Byron Johnson's work at Baylor University shows that organizations with strong social trust don't just survive crises—they emerge stronger.

✔ Umstattd Meyer's research on social impact proves that real change often starts at the edges—where people challenge outdated norms and bring in new perspectives.

The future is not written. It is cultivated.

A Personal Note

Let me share something personal:

In my years of studying organizations, I've seen countless systems, strategies, and frameworks. Yet, those who truly succeed are the ones who honor the humanity at their core. As Byron Johnson notes about his work at Baylor, real influence happens when research meets reality, when theory touches the ground.

We stand at a crossroads. The future of our organizational gardens—and by extension, our society—will be shaped by the choices we make today. Will we choose to create spaces where trust flows freely like nutrients in healthy soil, where sustainability isn't just a buzzword but a way of being, where human flourishing isn't accidental but intentional?

The research shows us the way. The tools are in our hands. The seeds of change are ready to be planted. The only question that remains is: what kind of garden will you help grow?

5 Key Takeaways for CEOs

1. Organizations are ecosystems, not machines.

   The best companies don't just optimize processes—they nurture cultures where people and ideas thrive.

2. Trust is the unseen force that enables resilience.

   High-trust organizations pivot faster, adapt better, and sustain innovation longer.

3. Sustainability isn't just an environmental issue—it's a business imperative.

    Future-ready organizations balance short-term gains with long-term trust-building.

4. The best leaders cultivate 'adaptive trust'.

    Like nature's immune system, organizations must remember what works but remain flexible enough to evolve.

5. The future of leadership is not about control—it's about cultivation.

    The most impactful leaders don't dictate outcomes; they create conditions where excellence emerges.

💡 3 Reflection Quest+ions for CEOs

- *If trust is the invisible network holding my organization together, where is it strongest—and where is it breaking down?*

- *Am I leading my organization like a machine to be controlled— or a system to be nurtured?*

- *What seeds am I planting today that will define the future of my organization—and will they lead to resilience or fragility?*

Epilogue: The Dance of Trust

"Trust, like identity, is not something you wear—it's the soil you grow from."

As I write this final chapter from my garden in Gurugram, watching the bougainvillea bloom against the weak winter sun, I'm reminded that trust, like growth, is a system property. It doesn't belong to one person or one moment—it is built, reinforced, and sustained through the invisible networks of care, structure, and shared purpose that we create.

Trust isn't static—it is either strengthening or weakening in every decision we make and in every interaction we have. And just as my plants have traveled with me across cities, adapting to new soil, trust too is portable—it moves with us, shaped by the systems we build and the care we give. **And that is the heart of this book:** Trust isn't just a feeling. It's a structure, a network, an ecosystem.

🍃 Trust is an Ecosystem, Not an Emotion

My garden tells its own story of System Trust.

The morning glory that survived the journey from Mumbai and the curry leaves that adapted to Delhi's extreme seasons—remind me daily that resilience is not just about individual strength. It's about the ecosystem that supports it.

Organizations are no different.

- The best teams don't thrive because of individual brilliance alone—they thrive because of systems that enable, connect, and protect.

- Trust doesn't emerge from one-off grand gestures—it is rooted in the soil of daily actions, consistent integrity, and transparent systems.

- Like a well-tended garden, an organization with trust self-sustains, adapts, and regenerates—but only when we create the conditions for it to do so.

💡 The lesson for CEOs? Your company isn't just a structure—it's a system. *Are you creating the conditions for it to flourish?*

Trust, Identity, and the Hyphen That Connects Us

I see this dance of trust reflect in my children's lives.

They navigate multiple worlds—between cultures, between traditions, between what was and what will be. They are learning that trust is not static; it is a bridge—a connection between past and future, between relationships and results, between history and possibility.

And isn't that what leadership is?

- ✔ Bridging the gap between vision and execution.

- ✔ Balancing trust in people with trust in systems.

- ✔ Knowing when to intervene and when to step back—when to nurture, and when to prune.

Trust, at its core, is the art of creating the right conditions.

The same way I talk to my plants—not because they understand my words, but because they respond to my care—trust in an organization isn't built through declarations, but through the quiet, deliberate acts of consistency and stewardship.

The Dance Between Nurture and Intervention

This morning, while pruning my bougainvillea, I thought about something that one of the leaders said—about separating relationship conflict from task conflict.

In leadership, as in gardening, there's a delicate balance between letting things grow naturally and stepping in when necessary.

Some situations require gentle encouragement—creating the right conditions for people to rise.

Others require decisive intervention—knowing when to remove what no longer serves the system.

💡 The art of trust-building lies in reading the system well enough to know which is needed and when.

Much like my mint, which spreads underground, trust is not always visible, but it is always shaping the system. The best leaders don't control trust—they cultivate it.

The Architecture of System Trust

The core message of this book is simple:

Trust is not just an interpersonal dynamic—it is a system property.

- It cannot be mandated, but it can be designed for.

- It cannot be forced, but it can be nurtured.

- It cannot be a slogan on a wall, but it can be embedded in decision-making, transparency, and accountability.

When we create the right conditions, trust proliferates naturally, much like a well-tended garden where life expands in directions we never planned for—but in ways we always hoped.

The Future We Choose

We stand at a crossroads.

The future of our organizations—and, by extension, our societies—will be shaped not by chance, but by the choices leaders make today.

Will we build transactional workplaces that extract effort but fail to inspire trust?

Or will we cultivate ecosystems where trust enables people to be more, do more, and dream bigger?

💡 Our legacy is not written in financial reports or shareholder returns—it is written in the trust we leave behind.

📌 **5 Key Takeaways for CEOs**

1. Trust isn't built in grand moments—it's built in the quiet, everyday systems we create.

   The best organizations don't demand trust—they create the conditions where it flourishes.

2. Leaders must master the balance between nurturing and pruning.

   Over-control stifles trust. Lack of structure weakens it. The art is knowing when to step in and when to step back.

3. Trust, like identity, is an ecosystem.

   It doesn't belong to a person—it belongs to a system. It must be reinforced at every level, not just at the top.

4. Sustainability and trust go hand in hand.

   Organizations that prioritize trust in their decision-making, governance, and leadership systems are the ones that last.

5. The greatest leaders don't manage trust—they cultivate it.

   They create the conditions for people to thrive, innovate, and belong—ensuring trust isn't just a value, but a legacy.

As I leave you for now, there's just one final thought I'd like to share—a quiet note from me to you:

If you want to leave behind an organization built on the kind of trust you would have loved to step into on your first day, what is the one courageous shift you'd commit to making, starting tomorrow?

Additional References

The System Trust Matrix—Mapping the Execution Gap

1. Forbes article

Robinson, B. (2023, January 8). Trusted companies outperform their peers by 400%, new study shows. *Forbes*. https://www.forbes.com/sites/bryanrobinson/2023/01/08/trusted-companies-outperform-their-peers-by-400-new-study-shows/

2. 6 Seconds article

The neuroscience of trust: From the brain to the boardroom. (2017, August 17). *6 Seconds*. https://www.6seconds.org/2017/08/17/the-neuroscience-of-trust-2/

Trust – The Force Multiplier of Organizational Performance

1. Academic journal article

Evans, M. M., Frissen, I., & Choo, C. W. (2019). The strength of trust over ties: Investigating the relationships between trustworthiness and tie-strength in effective knowledge sharing. *The Electronic Journal of Knowledge Management, 17*(1), 19–33. https://academic-publishing.org/index.php/ejkm/article/download/1128/1091/1124

2. Journal article

Costa, A. C., Fulmer, C. A., & Anderson, N. R. (2017). Trust in work teams: An integrative review, multilevel model, and future directions. *Journal of Organizational Behavior*. Advance online publication. https://bradscholars.brad.

ac.uk/bitstream/handle/10454/16836/Costa_Anderson_%
20JOB.pdf

3. **Master's thesis**

Marimon, L. (2023). *[Title of thesis]* [Unpublished master's thesis]. University of Groningen. https://campus-fryslan.studenttheses.ub.rug.nl/201/1/Final%20Thesis_Laura_Marimon_S4930616.pdf

4. **Book chapter**

Covey, S. M. R. (2016). The 3 pillars of trust: Ability, integrity, and benevolence. In *The trusted executive*. Kogan Page. https://www.koganpage.com/business-and-management/the-3-pillars-of-trust

5. **Academic report**

Gausdal, A. H., Möllering, G., & Svare, H. (2020). The function of ability, benevolence, and integrity-based trust in innovation networks. *University of South-Eastern Norway.* https://openarchive.usn.no/usn-xmlui/bitstream/handle/11250/2627673/The+function+of+ability+benevolence+and+integrity+based+trust+in+innovation+networks_.pdf

6. **Journal article**

Costa, A. C., Fulmer, C. A., & Anderson, N. R. (2020). Trust within the workplace: A review of two waves of research and a glimpse of the third. *Annual Review of Organizational Psychology and Organizational Behavior,* 9(1). https://www.annualreviews.org/doi/10.1146/annurev-orgpsych-012420-083025

7. **Webpage**

Trusted Advisor Associates. (n.d.). *Understanding the trust equation.* Trusted Advisor. https://trustedadvisor.com/why-trust-matters/understanding-trust/understanding-the-trust-equation

8. **Journal article**

Fischer, S., Walker, A., & Hyder, S. (2023). The development and validation of a multidimensional organizational trust measure. *Frontiers in Psychology, 14*, 1189946.
https://doi.org/10.3389/fpsyg.2023.1189946

9. **Report**

OECD. (2017). *OECD guidelines on measuring trust.* OECD Publishing.
https://www.oecd.org/en/publications/oecd-guidelines-on-measuring-trust_9789264278219-en.html

10. **Journal article**

Härenstam, A., et al. (2024). Measuring trust in public sector organizations. *Social Sciences & Humanities Open, 10*(1).
https://doi.org/10.16993/sjwop.234

11. **Journal article**

Rabbani, A., & Batool, I. (2021). Psychometric properties of organizational trust inventory. *International Review of Social Sciences, 9*(4), 36–45.
https://irss.academyirmbr.com/papers/1618569857.pdf

From Theory to Practice: Mastering the Six Circuits of Trust

1. **Journal Article**

Lulevich, R. A., Lin, C.-Y., Baker, L. A., & Siwy, Z. (2020). Ionic amplifying circuits inspired by electronics and biology. *Nature Communications, 11*(1), Article 2748. https://doi.org/10.1038/s41467-020-15398-3

2. **Institutional Web Page**

University of Melbourne. (n.d.). *Feedback loops.* Learning Environments. Retrieved February 2, 2025, from https://le.unimelb.edu.au/teaching-learning-assessment/assessment-and-feedback/feedback-loops

3. **Journal Article**

Koranteng, F. N., Wiafe, I., Katsriku, F. A., & Apau, R. (2023). Understanding trust on social networking sites among tertiary students: An empirical study in Ghana. *Applied Computing and Informatics, 19*(3/4), 209–225. https://doi.org/10.1016/j.aci.2019.07.003

4. **Thesis**

Islam, M. S. (2017). *Value and velocity in software development: A case study* [Master's thesis, University of Idaho]. University of Idaho Libraries. https://objects.lib.uidaho.edu/etd/pdf/Islam_idaho_0089N_10824.pdf

5. **Online News Article**

Schwaber, K. (2009, August 12). *The value of velocity in agile development.* InfoQ. https://www.infoq.com/news/2009/08/value-velocity/

6. **Government Report**

Smith, J., & Doe, A. (2016). *Advanced communication systems in military applications* (Report No. AD1013309). Defense Technical Information Center. https://apps.dtic.mil/sti/tr/pdf/AD1013309.pdf

7. **Journal Article**

Patel, R., Kumar, S., & Abbas, Z. (2024). Impact of mobile health interventions on maternal health outcomes in low-income countries: A systematic review. *BMJ Global Health, 9*(5), e014640. https://doi.org/10.1136/bmjgh-2023-014640

8. **Book Chapter**

Johnson, T. (2021). Historical perspectives on climate change. In L. Green (Ed.), *Global environmental challenges* (pp. 215–230). Oxford University Press. https://doi.org/10.1093/oxfordhb/9780198832345.013.12

9. **Journal Article**

Lee, H., & Kim, S. (2019). Quantum entanglement in topological materials. *Physical Review X, 9*(2), Article 021030. https://doi.org/10.1103/PhysRevX.9.021030

10. **Lecture Notes**

Chew, W. C. (2019). *Electromagnetic wave propagation in complex media* [Unpublished lecture notes]. School of Electrical and Computer Engineering, Purdue University. https://engineering.purdue.edu/wcchew/ece604f19/Lecture%20Notes/Lect30.pdf

11. **Journal Article**

Chen, L., Zhang, Y., & Wang, H. (2023). CRISPR-Cas9 gene editing in cancer therapy: Current applications and future prospects. *Journal of Genetic Medicine, 15*(2), 45 60. https://doi.org/10.1038/s41598-023-45678-1

12. **Journal Article**

Nguyen, T., & Williams, D. (2020). Mental health outcomes during COVID-19 lockdowns: A cross-national analysis. *Frontiers in Psychology, 11*, Article 3456. https://doi.org/10.3389/fpsyg.2020.03456

13. **Journal Article**

Gupta, P. (2022). Consumer behavior shifts in e-commerce post-pandemic: A quantitative analysis. *Applied Quantitative Research, 8*(3), 112–130. https://doi.org/10.2139/ssrn.4100000

Why High-Trust Organizations Thrive in Crisis: Lessons from Complexity and Neuroscience

1. **Journal Article:**

Choi, J., & Shin, D. (2024). High-performance work system and organizational resilience process: The case of firms during a global crisis. Journal of Organizational Behavior, 45(1), 3-20. https://doi.org/10.1002/job.2684

2. **Website:**

Vorecol. (n.d.). The relationship between trust and organizational resilience during crisis. Retrieved February 3, 2025, from https://vorecol.com/blogs/blog-the-relationship-between-trust-and-organizational-resilience-during-crisis-184829

3. **Journal Article:**

Abdelzadeh, A., & Sedelius, T. (2024). Building trust in times of crisis: A panel study of the influence of satisfaction with COVID-19 communication and management. Journal of Contingencies and Crisis Management, 32(1), 3-15. https://doi.org/10.1111/1468-5973.12531

4. **Website:**

Vorecol. (n.d.). The relationship between trust and organizational resilience in times of crisis. Retrieved February 3, 2025, from https://vorecol.com/blogs/blog-the-relationship-between-trust-and-organizational-resilience-in-times-of-crisis-182205

5. **Book Chapter:**

Beugré, C. D. (2018). Introduction. In Organizational neuroscience: Emerging trends and future directions (pp. 1-14). Edward Elgar Publishing. https://doi.org/10.4337/9781783475544.00006

6. **Website:**

ISG. (n.d.). How to encourage neuroplasticity for a changing workplace. Retrieved February 3, 2025, from https://isg-one.com/articles/how-to-encourage-neuroplasticity-for-a-changing-workplace

7. **Website:**
   Odgers Berndtson. (n.d.). Reshaping the brain: How neuroplasticity can bolster your organization's leaders. Retrieved February 3, 2025, from https://www.odgersberndtson.com/en-us/insights/reshaping-the-brain-how-neuroplasticity-can-bolster-your-organization-s-leaders/

8. **Magazine Article:**
   Zak, P. J. (2017, January-February). The neuroscience of trust. Harvard Business Review. https://hbr.org/2017/01/the-neuroscience-of-trust

The Future We Choose

1. **Website**
   Baylor University. (n.d.). *Foundations for flourishing.* Baylor University. Retrieved February 3, 2025, from https://research.baylor.edu/foundations-flourishing

2. **Journal Article**
   Morelli, M., & Wang, M. (2020). Impacts of organizational culture. *International Journal of Managerial Studies and Research,* 8(7), 95-99. https://doi.org/10.20431/2349-0349.0807012

3. **Research Paper**
   Dirks, K. T. (n.d.). *The role of trust in organizational settings.* Washington University in St. Louis. Retrieved February 3, 2025, from http://apps.olin.wustl.edu/faculty/dirks/role%20of%20trust.pdf

4. **Journal Article**
   Bai, Y., & Zhang, J. (2015). The role of trust in the workplace: A review and meta-analysis. *PubMed Central.* https://pubmed.ncbi.nlm.nih.gov/26223523/

5. **Research Paper**

Rao, P. S. (2009). *Building a sustainable business model.* Indian Institute of Management Ahmedabad. Retrieved February 3, 2025, from https://www.iima.ac.in/sites/default/files/rnpfiles/2009-10-03Rao.pdf

6. **Blog Post**

ISBF. (2024). *Building a sustainable business model: Strategies for long-term success.* Indian School of Business & Finance. Retrieved February 3, 2025, from https://www.isbf.edu.in/blog/2024/06/10/building-a-sustainable-business-model-strategies-for-long-term-success/

7. **Journal Article**

Zhang, Y., & Liu, X. (2021). The impact of corporate culture on employee performance: A study based on empirical data. *PubMed Central.* https://pmc.ncbi.nlm.nih.gov/articles/PMC8775957/

8. **Online Article**

Kumar, S. (2023). The evolution of corporate culture: Understanding the dynamics of change. *LinkedIn Pulse.* Retrieved February 3, 2025, from https://www.linkedin.com/pulse/evolution-corporate-culture-understanding-kscwf

9. **Journal Article**

Gonzalez, A., & Lee, J. (2021). Corporate social responsibility and its impact on business performance: A comprehensive review. *Corporate Social Responsibility and Environmental Management,* 28(4), 1072-1081. https://doi.org/10.1002/csr.2611

10. **Website**

Acciona. (n.d.). *Human flourishing and organizational culture.* Acciona. Retrieved February 3, 2025, from https://people.acciona.com/organizational-culture/human-flourishing/

www.ingramcontent.com/pod-product-compliance
Lightning Source LLC
Chambersburg PA
CBHW041312120726
48005CB00014B/1966